Jackie Kendall

a **man** worth waiting for

how to avoid a bozo

D0109766

 New York Boston Nashville

Copyright © 2008 by Jackie Kendall

All rights reserved. Except as permitted under the U.S. Copyright Act of 1976, no part of this publication may be reproduced, distributed, or transmitted in any form or by any means, or stored in a database or retrieval system, without the prior written permission of the publisher.

Unless otherwise noted, Scriptures are taken from the HOLY BIBLE: NEW INTERNATIONAL VERSION®. Copyright © 1973, 1978, 1984 by International Bible Society. Used by permission of Zondervan Publishing House. All rights reserved.
Scriptures noted NLT are from the *Holy Bible*, New Living Translation, copyright © 1996. Used by permission of Tyndale House Publishers, Inc., Wheaton, Illinois 60189. All rights reserved.
Scriptures marked KJV are from the King James Version of the Bible.
Scriptures noted ESV are taken from The Holy Bible, English Standard Version, copyright © 2001 by Crossway Bibles, a division of Good News Publishers. Used by permission. All rights reserved.
Scriptures noted NKJV are taken from the NEW KING JAMES VERSION. Copyright © 1979, 1980, 1982, Thomas Nelson, Inc., Publishers.

FaithWords
Hachette Book Group USA
237 Park Avenue
New York, NY 10017

Visit our Web site at www.faithwords.com.

Printed in the United States of America

First Edition: March 2008
10 9 8 7 6 5 4 3 2 1

FaithWords is a division of Hachette Book Group USA, Inc.
The FaithWords name and logo is a trademark of Hachette Book Group USA, Inc.

Library of Congress Cataloging-in-Publication Data

Kendall, Jackie, 1950–
     A man worth waiting for : how to avoid a bozo / Jackie Kendall. — 1st ed.
        p. cm.
     ISBN-13: 978-0-446-69971-6
     ISBN-10: 0-446-69971-3
     1. Mate selection. 2. Women—Psychology. 3. Dating (Social customs)—Religious aspects—Christianity. 4. Man-woman relationships—Religious aspects—Christianity. I. Title.
     HQ801.K457 2008
     241'.6765082—dc22
                                                    2007010688

Praise for *A MAN WORTH WAITING FOR*

"Jackie Kendall's follow-up to *Lady in Waiting* speaks intimately to faithful single women in the voice of our loving Father. She reminds all of us to be true to ourselves, to trust in God's plan and perfect timing, and most importantly, not to settle for anything less than God's best—ever!"

—Kristin Armstrong, author of
*Happily Ever After: Walking with Peace and
Courage Through a Year of Divorce*

"Jackie Kendall gets the world you struggle in, and she gets *you*. Even more amazing, she shows you, with the rockin' power she is known for on the speaking platform, how to live in that real world in purity, in passion, in love with Jesus Christ. Forget the bookmark—you won't put this one down."

—Nancy Rue, award-winning author of 105 books for girls

"In a culture that encourages women to put more effort into finding the right pair of jeans over the right kind of man, it's no wonder relationships are failing. Jackie Kendall has penned a must-read manual for every single woman who refuses to settle for less than God's best when it comes to a future mate."

—Vicki Courtney, bestselling author and founder of
Virtuous Reality Ministries

"While there's no such thing as the 'perfect man' (just as you will never be the 'perfect woman') and only Jesus Christ can truly be the 'knight in shining armor'—our Messiah who saves the damsel in distress—the man you choose in life can either make you or break you from being the woman of God you are intended to be. I love Jackie's candid, laced-with-humor style of conveying truth to help you avoid the Bozos in the minefield of matrimony. This book will be required reading for my three daughters."

—Lisa Ryan, Christian TV host,
speaker, and author of *For Such a Time as This*

"I was single until I was thirty-nine and married my Boaz nine years ago. I have lived many of the principles in the book as I heard Jackie speak about them in 1982. The principles are consistent with sound counseling principles and I have seen how they have helped many women in my counseling ministry. I wholeheartedly recommend the book."

—Dr. Elizabeth Skjoldal, associate professor,
Trinity International University

To Ken Kendall,
my Boaz

contents

acknowledgments ix

introduction xi

part I your choices defined: bozo or boaz

1 the original MWWF: boaz 3

2 is the man worth waiting for (MWWF) an extinct
ideal? 11

3 the counterfeit of a man worth waiting for: bozo 29

part II the essential elements of a MWWF

4 farmers and princes 47

5 sexual and holy 71

6 emotional maturity 89

7 courage in suffering 107

8 reckless abandon 119

9 faithful though flawed 137

10 surrounded by good company 158

part III **your role in locating a MWWF**

11 don't be bozo bait 179

12 be kind to your heart 199

a final note: who is writing your love story? 217

notes 221

about the author 224

acknowledgments

On September 16, 2005, I prayed that the next decade of my life would be the most fruitful. This book is a specific answer to that prayer. Thank You, Jesus, for such extravagant grace given to this warrior of the cross. And thanks to:

Holly Halverson, who took my book from good to great for the glory of our heavenly Bridegroom.

Ruth A. Olsen, my priceless writing mentor. This book would not exist without your compassionate critique of my ponderings.

Sami Cone, whose research, combined with hours of sorting all the questionnaire responses, was invaluable.

Leslie Nunn Reed, the most awesome literary agent—whose calm guidance was invaluable.

So many women, young and old, who have shared their painful stories about their Bozo experiences.

All those who participated in the questionnaire, especially: Jessi, Drew Sr., George, Tipton, Tim, Chad, Cody, Eddie, David, John, Mike, Gary, Chuck, Whit, Dan, Jennie, Alicia, Victoria, Barb, Ana, Kathy, Renee, Ashley, Keren, Linda, Fred, Sue, Susan, Chris, Steve, Tom, Nichole, Jim, Terry, Emmary, O.S., Lisa, Garrett, Kimberly, and Jonathan.

Major thanks to BWK (my firstborn son) for hours of processing thoughts about the twenty-first-century male; my son-in-law, Drew, who is such an inspiration as a twenty-first-century Boaz; and Cody McQueen for extensive and priceless comments on the ideal man. Doug Rose and Doug Chapple— what a gift your input was. Thanks to Jennie Clay, for her candid remarks about Internet dating.

I'm so grateful for my family—Ken, Ben, Jessi, and Drew— who were so supportive while I was on a book sabbatical, and last but not least, for the prayers of so many friends (especially Bettye, DeDe, and Victoria), which allowed me to pour my heart into print with absolute freedom and joy.

introduction

have seen too many women pass school but fail life. I have met thousands of single women who are very intentional about becoming the best they can be—but they seem to be unsuccessful in finding a man who is striving to be godly. For more than three decades, I have been repeating one phrase so incessantly that it is a wonder that people have not come after me with duct tape. I not only have taught it as a constant theme, but I also have signed countless copies of *Lady in Waiting* with this remark: "Wait for God's best and avoid a Bozo!"

Why does a brilliant woman say "I do" to a jerk? How does a woman with two doctorates pick two terrible husbands? How does a woman who's shown exquisite taste and high standards in every area of her life choose a man who will bring her nothing but heartache?

I am knee-deep in a pool of tears from those women who have chosen poor dates and mates. After three decades of listening to thousands of women sharing their heartbreaking experiences with loser guys, I decided to write about the characteristics of the man who is the opposite.

How did I find him? On yet another dateless Friday night in 1972, I met this man in my college dorm room in the greatest book ever printed on the Gutenberg press. I discovered the ideal man in the eighth book of the Old Testament, Ruth. His name is Boaz. He is the opposite of what I call a Bozo, a guy who breaks a woman's heart and leaves her wondering if there is any alternative to this type of man in the universe. In my book *Lady in Waiting,* I gave readers a glimpse of a Man Worth Waiting For. This book will be the full-color portrait of him.

I believe in the power of guidebooks. For our thirtieth anniversary, friends gave us a two-week trip to Europe. Yes, this was an extravagant gift. One of our dear friends gave us an invaluable gift for our time in Paris. She made a little book with details that covered *every* aspect of *every moment* of our time in Paris.

She included maps to the places we could walk to for breakfast, lunch, and dinner; tips on saving money by going to various museums on certain days and times; pictures of the places we were going to see; the best times to travel to beat the mobs of tourists; directions to the best restaurants; and even what trains to ride and when it would be the wisest to get a taxi.

The details went on for pages and were arranged by days. She knew what we wanted to see and what we were not interested in. She even included, in case we got lost, a card with the address of where we were staying—so we could just show someone the card. The book was tailor-made for us.

This guidebook kept us from so many potential traveling disasters and afforded us the richest of experiences in Paris. People marveled at all we saw in such a short amount of time. We always say, "We had a personal guide 24/7." When we arrived in Prague, the first thing we noted was how we wished we had another guidebook like the one our dear friend made for our time in Paris.

This book is my heart's guidebook for you as you maneuver the streets of romance. I want to help you avoid the unnecessary heartache awaiting the unsuspecting woman in Bozo Alley. This guidebook to avoid the Bozos out there is the result of thirty-one years of marriage, twenty-six years of parenting, and thirty-nine years of ministry. I believe I have lived and observed enough to write this guidebook.

Personally, when I was younger, I was a girl destined to marry a Bozo. I didn't know any other type of man existed. I was raised in an abusive home that revolved around a man full of grandiose entitlement. I learned young what a man could evolve into if he were allowed to believe that the whole world existed to serve him.

My father's passionate commitment to self-indulgence left me wondering. For years I pondered the question: *Are all men outside our home just another version of the first man in my life?* My life could have been a textbook example of dysfunction begetting dysfunction, grooming me for a Bozo in a life partner.

Then a spiritual mentor said, "Jackie, you can learn more from a 'good bad example' than you can from many good examples." My father was a painful example of what I did not want to spend the rest of my life with. When my mentor said that, my heart felt a glimmer of hope that I could learn from my relationship with my dad and that I would someday find a man who was the opposite of my father.

Little did I know that on a dateless Friday night, in a college dorm room, I would read about a man who was so captivating and so inspiring that I had finally found the contrast—in the Bible of all places. More about this later; for now, suffice it to say that on that dateless Friday night, a man named Boaz became the healing example that gave my heart a clear view of what God intended a man to be like.

That night Boaz surpassed all the romantic heroes that I had dreamed about through years of movies, books, and TV shows; that night I received a clear picture of a Man Worth Waiting For.

One time I was talking to a nurse, telling her my life story, and when she heard about my extremely dysfunctional family she said, "It is amazing to think that someone from your background would pick such an awesome man to marry." Because of the clear example provided by Boaz, it was a very obvious choice to me whom I should marry.

During the last eleven years of traveling the nation and teaching about relationships, I kept meeting scores of women who chose the Bozo guy I had warned about in my book *Lady in Waiting*. The Bozo Tribe membership is at an all-time high. These guys are exploiting some of the most amazing women—women who have often passed school but are flunking life.

If you are a woman who is getting over Mr. Wrong, or a woman who is waiting for Mr. Right, I hope this book is challenging as well as a burst of fresh oxygen for your soul. I hope women will see Boaz as a classic example of a man worth the wait—even if that means decades of waiting.

If, after reading these pages, you feel more of an "ouch" than an "amen," I hope you will look to the Commander of a million stars, God Almighty, to give you the strength to abandon the Bozo Tribe for a Boaz—A Man Worth Waiting For.

part I

your choices defined

bozo or boaz

❀ Throughout this book, we will look at the qualities of a Man Worth Waiting For. In this first section we'll focus on the Old Testament character Boaz as a prime example of the guy you need to look for. We will compare Boaz to his glaring opposite, the Bozo who keeps successfully exploiting so many wonderful women. A prince named Amnon is the best example of a Bozo in biblical record, and I'll tell you more about him in the pages to come.

❀ 1

the original MWWF: boaz

Before Tristan and Isolde, before Romeo and Juliet, and even before Mr. Darcy and Miss Elizabeth of *Pride and Prejudice*, there were Boaz and Ruth. Their love story, dating from approximately 1000 BC, is still powerfully relevant in the twenty-first century.

Boaz, the leading man in the Hebrew book of Ruth, enters this short love story in chapter 2. This book is the story of a young widow named Ruth, whose heart had been broken by her husband's death yet healed by faith in the God of Israel. Having touched God's heart, she also touched the heart of one of God's champion followers—Boaz. The intersection of their lives becomes not only the framework of an earthly love story but also the foreshadowing of the greatest love story, God's love for the world through Jesus—Himself a descendant of the union of Boaz and Ruth.

After we look at their story, we'll look at how it affects your story today. Granted, this story has some odd twists and turns unfamiliar to our twenty-first-century minds, but solid principles are there as well.

An Ancient Love Story: Boaz and Ruth

Ruth, as I've mentioned, was a young widow. After her husband's death, she chose to continue living with her former mother-in-law, Naomi, also widowed, who believed in the God of Israel. Ruth was a Moabitess—a foreigner who did not follow the Hebrew God. Yet when she opted to remain Naomi's companion, she stated, "Where you go I will go, and where you stay, I will stay. Your people will be my people and your God my God" (Ruth 1:16). She swore her allegiance to the lonely older woman, who was heartbroken over the total loss of her family. The two traveled from Moab to Naomi's home in Bethlehem just as the harvest of barley was starting.

These women had no men to provide for them, but Ruth was enterprising, and she suggested she glean in the fields behind the barley harvesters. God had commanded that landowners leave anything harvesters didn't pick up so the poor, the widowed, the foreigners, and the fatherless had a supply of food (Lev. 19:9–10). Ruth just so happened to glean in a field owned by a man named Boaz—a relative of Naomi's dead husband, no less.

Enter Boaz

When Boaz came out to see how the harvesters fared, he noticed Ruth and asked about her. Learning that she was a hard worker, he pulled her aside and told her to glean alongside his servant girls. There, she—young, foreign, and alone—would be safe from possible molesters among the harvesters. And Boaz gave Ruth freedom to drink from his water jars as she worked.

This was extraordinary treatment! Ruth was stunned and asked why the man gave with such kindness. Boaz responded that he had heard of Ruth's devotion to Naomi, how she left her homeland to be companion to her weary mother-in-law. And he admired her newfound faith in the God of Israel. Boaz blessed Ruth, saying, "May you be richly rewarded by the LORD, the God of Israel, under whose wings you have come to take refuge" (Ruth 2:12).

He went on then to feed her from his own table and to make sure his harvesters left behind choice grain for her to pick up.

Naomi Has an Idea

Naomi suggested that Ruth act on the custom of the day, which allowed the young woman to call upon her nearest male relative to serve as her kinsman-redeemer. A kinsman-redeemer would buy back Ruth and Naomi's dead husbands' land as well as become Ruth's new husband.

As instructed, Ruth went one evening to the threshing floor where Boaz and his men were working. When Boaz lay down that night, Ruth uncovered his feet and lay down near him. In the middle of the night he awoke, saw her, and asked who she was.

"I am your servant Ruth," she said. "Spread the corner of your garment over me, since you are a kinsman-redeemer" (Ruth 3:9).

Again Boaz reacted kindly to Ruth, blessing her and noting that she did not "run after the younger men, whether rich or poor." He assured her, "Don't be afraid. . . . All my fellow townsmen know that you are a woman of noble character" (Ruth 3:10–11). He promised to act on her request.

Boaz Acts Honorably

One rule stood in the way: Ruth had one nearer male relative who had first rights to buy the land that belonged to her as part of the family of Elimelech, Naomi's husband. Boaz, a fair man, said he would give this man his opportunity to buy the land and marry Ruth.

Long story short, the man was interested in the land but not Ruth, so he opted out of both. Boaz and Ruth were married, and they later produced the forebear of David—who was the forebearer of Jesus.

All the World Is Blessed

That this is a love story with eternal impact reveals why the book of Ruth was read each year to the children of Israel during the feasts of Israel.[1] It reminded them that their Lord was their Boaz: their pillar of strength, their trustworthy, forever Bridegroom. Isaiah the prophet wrote, "For your Maker is your husband, the LORD Almighty is His name" (Isa. 54:5).

Boaz Then and Now

Let's look now at what this story tells us today about men—
what to hope for, what a good man will act like, and why he's
worth waiting for.

A Boaz Respects You

In the third chapter of this love story, Ruth approached Boaz
with the request that he become her kinsman-redeemer. This
was not the bold move of an impatient single woman. This was
a request guided by Naomi, who understood the legal obliga-
tions of family based on Deuteronomy 25:5–10.

Boaz was surprised and pleased by Ruth's request. His godly
character and respect show in his reply to her request: "The
LORD bless you, my daughter. . . . I will do for you all you ask"
(Ruth 3:10–11).

In short, this exchange tells us that if a man won't speak and
act respectfully toward you, he's a Bozo.

A Boaz Respects the Law

Boaz obeyed the law God gave in Deuteronomy. He didn't grab
what wasn't his; he wasn't sneaky. Instead he openly respected
the law and his relative. And he won the bride!

A Boaz Will Handle Your "Baggage" with Care

Boaz as the kinsman-redeemer was not only willing to buy the
land that had belonged to Ruth's dead husband, but he was
also willing to honor the name of the dead husband when he
married Ruth. The cost, financially and emotionally, did not
cause Boaz to hesitate. Ruth 4 reveals that another relative was

a close kinsman. But this relative was not willing to accept the "baggage" that came with marrying Ruth—therefore, Boaz was granted the privilege of being Ruth's kinsman-redeemer.

Remember, Ruth was a Moabitess, a member of Israel's enemy tribe. Boaz enthusiastically married a woman from the wrong side of the tracks who had financial and emotional needs.

Of course, all women bring needs into a marriage. When it comes to God's best for a woman, it involves so much more than just a great guy. A Man Worth Waiting For is a man who can handle your particular baggage.

For example, my Boaz had to handle the "baggage" I brought to our marriage: the impact of a very dysfunctional family and sexual abuse. Not just any man could handle such heavy "luggage." God knew the man who had enough faith to patiently love me while Jesus and I sorted through my past emotional and physical wounds.

Boaz was a symbol of Jesus as our ultimate Kinsman-Redeemer, who brought us back from the enemy of our souls. Jesus, like a Boaz, can handle the baggage of our lives and He alone knows the best man to handle all of our wounds without becoming bitter or resentful.

A Boaz Notices More Than Just Beauty

We see that Boaz noticed Ruth among all the harvesters and those who gleaned after the harvesters. We don't know how many people that entailed, but we know she stood out. The Bible tells us she was known for more than her looks; remember how he said, "All my fellow townsmen know that you are a woman of noble character" (Ruth 3:11)?

When one Boaz, a guy named Ben, first noticed an attractive single girl, they were sitting at their local singles' meeting. He saw that she was nodding as they listened to a great speaker. This Boaz said to his roommates who were at the Bible study with him, "I bet that girl is a P-31 [code for a 'Proverbs 31 woman']," and they asked, "How can you tell?" He replied, "I have noticed that she nods when the speaker makes some deeper remarks. Her nods showed she was tracking with him and really hungry for the truth." Later, he discovered that this P-31 woman's name was, ironically, Ruth.

During their first lengthy phone call, they told each other their life stories. As Ruth was sharing what she does and her passion to teach young people to choose the best by staying pure sexually, Ben realized that he needed to share with Ruth about his mom's ministry. So, in the middle of the conversation, Ben blurted out, "You need to meet my mom! You have the same vision and passion."

Ben recognized the heart of his own mom in a young woman. Consequently, I met Ruth and she ended up with me in a speaking ministry with Virtuous Reality. A modern Ruth was discovered by the son of a woman who wrote a book about Ruth (*Lady in Waiting*)! Ruth had never read my book, which totally shocked Ben, because Ruth lived the very principles that I wrote about.

A woman declares her heart even through a simple nod during a Bible study. She also declares her heart when she shares what she is passionate about. To a Boaz, a passionate heart is captivating in the way that a low-cut blouse is captivating to a Bozo! Boazes look for more than looks.

A side note: Most people are aware of the chapter in Proverbs that describes the ideal woman—the one my son referred to. The chapter says, "A wife of noble character who can find? She is worth far more than rubies" (Prov. 31:10). When I started thinking about the ideal husband/man, I thought the description should start this way: "Who can find a virtuous man? His price is far above *diamonds*!"

The Word of God has one chapter describing the virtuous woman—Proverbs 31—but I wonder if the preceding thirty chapters of Proverbs do not describe the virtuous man. We could call The Man Worth Waiting For a "Proverbs 1–30" man. Let's look at him more closely next.

DISCUSSION QUESTIONS

- ✿ How did you feel as you read Ruth's story? How did you feel when you "met" Boaz for the first time? How does their story affect you today?
- ✿ What are your favorite qualities that a Boaz would embody?
- ✿ Discuss the idea of a man's handling a woman's "baggage." Is this an unrealistic expectation? Do you have any baggage?
- ✿ List a few verses from Proverbs that describe an ideal man.
- ✿ What encourages you to hold out for a Boaz?

❧ 2

is the man worth waiting for (MWWF) an extinct ideal?

In a famous chick-liberation flick, one of the lead characters, Thelma, was sharing how she had accepted her painful lot in life. The other leading lady, Louise, an amateur philosopher, said, "You get what you settle for." Wow, did Louise tell Thelma!

The following e-mail sounds as if Thelma could have written it, and when I received it recently, it fired up my heart.

> I am so confused. . . . [My boyfriend] and the pastor are telling me that God wants us to get married because we've had sex, because God loves when we keep our word, and because it would be a good testimony of God's love to other people (not giving up etc.) . . . but I don't love him. I have realized that recently. I don't want to marry some-

one like him. He has not treated me well. . . . He has not protected my sexuality or my emotions. *How can God want us to get married?*

I am so scared here. Please help me. This is a huge decision, and I don't want to miss the opportunity to marry [this guy] if he is, in fact, God's Best for me! I don't want God to be angry with me for disobeying because my heart is broken and it hurts too much to continue!

I feel so dark and hopeless right now. Please write soon.

Notice the last adjectives in this e-mail: "dark" and "hopeless." Those are the perfect descriptions of the nightmare women experience when they settle for a Bozo. Here is another single girl tied up in the knots that are so characteristic of an unholy entanglement with a Bozo. Beneath her pain I can hear her crying, "Is this guy the best God has for me? Is there really a Man Worth Waiting For?"

Is Boaz Only an Illusion?

I wonder if the incessant parade of Bozos has not subconsciously convinced most women that the ideal man does not exist except in the movies or romantic novels. On the *Today* show, two bachelors were interviewed because they had been traveling the nation in search of the keys to a long-term, happy marriage. These men were interviewing only couples who had been married longer than forty years and who described themselves as "reasonably happy." Their favorite couple interviewed thus far shared the three keys to their "happily ever after" marriage: "1. Commitment 2. Commitment 3. Commitment."

I just smiled. I knew that the ideal man is capable of living these three keys: commitment, commitment, and commitment. Why am I so sure? Because the ideal man that we will examine in this book has the *character* to support such a commitment. A Bozo, on the other hand, may declare with great bravado that he is committed to the love of his life, but he will not be able to go the distance because he lacks the character mandatory for long-term, committed love.

I am here to tell you that *yes*, there are Men Worth Waiting For, and *yes*—they are worth the wait. Boaz was just one, but many have followed! I'll prove it to you in the pages of this book. We'll study not just the characteristics of a modern-day Boaz but how to recognize him—and his counterfeit—when you find him.

Why Wait? Wisdom Says So

One forty-six-year-old single woman commented that Prince Charming had not yet shown up—and she conjectured why: "The dashing young knight on his snow-white steed, who was going to ride into my life and sweep me off my feet, has apparently gotten lost in the forest."

True, he may take his time coming, but Prince Charming—a Man Worth Waiting For—is *always* worth the wait. Why? The Bible explains.

Wait Because the Days Are Evil—Bozos Abound

Fairy tales become nightmares in the arms of a Bozo. Maybe a Bozo has already broken your heart. There is nothing more frustrating for me than to hear about another nightmare caused by a girl's accepting the attention and affection of a Bozo. The next time you see a single girl beginning to carelessly doze into a Bozo daydream, shake her hard, throw water in her face, and yell, "Wake up! No Bozo nightmare for you!"

And if the person drifting into daydreams is you—be all the more forceful. Look at what Paul wrote: " 'Wake up, O sleeper' . . . Be very careful, then, how you live—not as unwise but as wise, making the most of every opportunity, because the days are evil" (Eph. 5:14–15). For singles, the fact that the "days are evil" means the Bozo Tribe is increasing across the planet. Too many daydreaming girls are going to be slipping into nightmares. Don't let this be you.

Wait Because You Can't Change a Bozo into a Boaz

If there is any lie that Bozo-dating women perpetually tell themselves, it is *I will change him. I will influence him so positively that he will become the man of my dreams.* I have met countless miserable married women who married Bozos in hopes of transforming them into Boazes.

Such self-talk is deceiving, and it is not unique. Even in the Torah, such deception within one's own mind was not uncommon. Look at Deuteronomy 29:19: "Let none of those who hear the warnings for this curse consider themselves immune, thinking, 'I am safe, even though I am walking in my own stubborn way' " (NLT).

Too many women stubbornly invest in relationships with Bozos anticipating that they will eventually have peace in the arms of their ideal mates. They openly disregard the good counsel of God, friends, and family, cursing themselves with denial. What a price they pay. Only God can make a Boaz out of a Bozo. Your love and commitment will never be enough to change a man from the inside out.

Wait Because You Can't Attract a Boaz Until You're a Ruth

One day I was listening to Dr. Laura Schlessinger counsel a concerned father on the radio about the Bozo his daughter was dating. He said the guy wasn't exactly a knight in shining armor. Then Dr. Laura said something painful but profound: "Sir, your daughter is seeking the level she is at." I have said the same thing to many parents who are upset about the people their children are dating. I always say, "We attract what we are." Your latest steady date is a reflection of your own heart.

If you find only Bozos attracted to you, it's time to investigate. What keeps you from catching a Boaz's eye? You can't attract what you aren't yourself.

The Ideal Man Defined

Not long ago, I sent out a questionnaire to get a random sampling of men's and women's views on the ideal man. Throughout this book, I will be sharing comments in more detail from the many respondents. Those who participated were married, divorced, and single. They came from all over the U.S. and a few from outside. Their ages, life circumstances, occupations, and spiritual conditions were varied, yet their responses had so many similarities. My questionnaire reminded me again that the qualities that make up a good man are not obsolete—as so many forces in this culture would have us believe.

Here is one of my favorite replies. This woman is a phenomenon to me. She is so tenacious that after contracting the West Nile virus two weeks before she was going to run the Ironman Race, and though deathly sick, she still ran the race and actually managed to finish it in a great time. I gave her the nickname Ironwoman Walker. She married a wonderful Boaz named Chad in January 2006. Of the thousands of singles I have known, Jennie totally embodied a woman intentional enough to scale the challenging mountain of waiting to find her Mr. Right.

> In your opinion, what are the top three characteristics that an ideal godly man should embody?
> 1. Godly wisdom
> 2. Humility
> 3. [He should be] *normal*. This may sound shallow, but it meant so much to me—a man who was not socially awkward, could hold his own, didn't smell, was comfortable with himself and God. After going on my first date with Chad, I loved being able to see *he was normal*. Many Christian guys I dated in the past were not normal—they were rather odd men of faith.

Have you ever felt that way? Bozos tend to be "odd." You know them when you see them.

I received a survey response from a man named Doug Chapple. Doug is in the know about men—young and old. His career of teaching and coaching for forty-five years sets him apart in his perspective about men and their ideals. Furthermore, Doug was single until he was fifty-three. Fourteen years later, he says he still feels as if he is on his honeymoon!

Look at what he has to say about godly men.

> In your opinion, what are the top qualities in an ideal man?
>
> An ideal man:
>
> ✛ should have a passion for the quality of gentleness.
>
> ✛ should desire to crawl up into the lap of Jesus and abide there minute by minute each day.
>
> ✛ should have a passion to be more Christlike in word, deed, and thought every minute of the day.
>
> ✛ should be one who desires to control his tongue with the help of the Holy Spirit.
>
> ✛ has a real desire for spiritual wisdom.
>
> ✛ is one who recognizes that he is of great importance/ significance to God and therefore he cares for/loves himself in such a manner that he is able to love others as himself.
>
> ✛ works to protect his heart and keep it open to the Holy Spirit and input from other brothers and sisters in Jesus.

Doug's list is a wonderful description of a MWWF. Let me share a summary of questionnaire responses to these same questions.

> Top Three Ideal Qualities, Male Respondents:
> 1. Integrity/humility
> 2. Honest
> 3. Servant leader

Other qualities listed:

Character

Empathy

Spiritual growth

Patience

Self-sacrifice

Teachable

Trustworthy

Top Three Qualities, Female Respondents:

1. Loving
2. Committed to God
3. Honest

Other qualities listed:

Confident

Leadership

Sense of humor

Communicator

Growing faith

Humility

Passionate

Hardworking

Listener

Servant's heart

What are your own top three qualities in a man? Can you define what you're really looking for?

If I had a chance to submit my questionnaire to the greatest Christian single man who ever lived, here is what Paul the apostle would have included in his response (Paul would not have been able to stop with three!):

An ideal man is:

1. Above reproach
2. Self-controlled
3. Wise
4. Respectable
5. Hospitable
6. Able to teach
7. Not addicted to wine
8. Not harsh or abrupt
9. Gentle
10. Not quarrelsome
11. Free from the love of money
12. A good manager of his own household
13. Not a new convert
14. A man with a good reputation among those who don't know Jesus (See 1 Tim. 3:2–7)

Good News: Men Seek Strong Role Models

My survey told me that men are as passionate about being good men as women are to find them! Boazes care about character. Look at the answers men gave to these questions:

Where do you look for your ideals as a man?
> Bible
> Jesus
> King David
> Paul the apostle
> Men who live what they believe
> Pastors
> Dad

Biographies
Upstanding people in the church

What characteristics are you still striving to achieve in
your personal walk with God?

1. Consistency
2. Patience
3. Acceptance of others
4. Contentment
5. Choosing God's way over the world's
6. Focus
7. Purity/avoiding lust
8. Transparency
9. Willing to admit mistakes

Look at a couple of other responses:

I look to men . . . [I] see living with purpose, vision,
and integrity. It's great to look to men of the Bible, especially Jesus, but to be honest, nothing fires me up
more . . . than a thirty-three-year-old man I [actually]
see loving his wife and kids and living sacrificially for
the kingdom.—*Douglas W. Rose, Campus Outreach staff,
Virginia Tech*

1. Integrity is the first thing that comes to mind. What
   you see is what you get. He is the same person with
   his family, on his job, with his friends . . . he is consistent. Doesn't have anything to hide from the Lord.

2. Wisdom. Very difficult thing to come by, because wisdom is from the Lord. Many people have knowledge, and it sounds good, but it isn't right. When we have wisdom from the Lord, we will always find God's best.

3. Humility. If a man has integrity and wisdom, there will always be people who want him. When that happens, it is easy to get caught up in ourselves, and fall prey to the three G's: the glory, the glitter, and the girls. The first two strengths then become a weakness, because he robs God of His glory.—*Mike Singletary, NFL Hall of Famer and professional football coach*

Interesting, isn't it? The survey results tell me that Boazes—men who want to and do reflect these wonderful qualities—are alive and well.

While reading the wonderful book *Marriable: Taking the Desperate Out of Dating*, I came upon a list that made me smile because it confirmed yet again that Boazes exist in the twenty-first century. It delineates well what a Boaz acts like in a dating situation:

A Gentleman:

❦ never asks her out for a date less than three days before said date.

❦ always picks her up at the front door for the date.

❦ isn't late picking her up.

❦ doesn't complain when she isn't ready when he gets there.

❦ has a plan for the evening and is prepared for changes in weather and/or activity.

❦ never asks her to pay for the date.

- ✿ doesn't check out other women when he's with her.
- ✿ doesn't stare at her assorted body parts.
- ✿ always calls after the date to tell her he had a good time.
- ✿ doesn't apologize for being a man.[1]

Such considerate behavior is not merely the result of a guy's having this list posted to his bathroom mirror. This type of behavior flows from a capacity that parallels the character of the man. Sustaining such unselfish behavior must be fueled by a principled character. A Bozo may be able to do a couple of things on this list, but he will be playing at chivalry, hoping to get his sexual appetite satisfied. A Boaz, however, behaves this way naturally because it's who he is.

Proof Positive

A single mom who resisted settling for a Bozo saw her patience pay off in marriage to a prince of a man. This is what she wrote on her questionnaire:

> God has used my darling to teach me what *grace* is! Never in any previous relationships has [a man] loved me "just as I am"—the way God created me to be. Doug has a tender, gentle, and thoughtful spirit in any interaction we have. He gently corrects, encourages, and guides. He seems to always know when I have to be reeled in if I am charging ahead of myself or anyone. Doug has the ability to be focused, "blade to the ground," yet willing to [hear] my input if I disagree with him.

Doug was ever so tender with his mother. You can see how this carried through in the way in which he loves and cares for me. His gentleness is a strength that few men have and a quality that [tells me] I am special, I count, I matter to him! —*Emmary, office manager*

Emmary's experience is exciting, isn't it? But wait, there's more!

Two of the sharpest single girls I have ever known attended a women's conference with me. During the conference, these young ladies were in discussion groups with married women. By the end of the session, the two singles were totally devastated. When they shared with me what they heard, they both began to tear up and express their heartache about so many women in such pathetic marriages. They asked, "Are there no good marriages out there besides yours, Jackie? Are there no more good guys left to marry? Are only Bozos available for us?"

I did my best to assure them that I believed that God had two precious Boaz guys for them . . . if they were willing to wait and continue to hope! Four years later, both of these young women are married to absolutely wonderful Boazes.

This can be you. Wait for him!

With a heart so fired up about encouraging women to not settle, I wrote this little poem:

Don't Settle
I hope you don't consider me to meddle,
When I say "Don't settle."
Have you heard my heart scream?
Don't give up your dream.

So many have settled for Prince Harming,
Rather than courageously wait for Prince Charming;
Settling for a Bozo,
Whose heart will be a no-show.
Despairing over your absent knight in shining armor
Will escort you into the arms of a carnival charmer.
Your Designer has dreamed much better for you,
Don't settle for a man who can't love you through and through.

—JMK

Make Him Climb, Girl

My friend Jennie mentored a group of college girls in California. She taught them a catchphrase for what men needed to do to win their hearts: "Make him climb a tree." The climbing would test his calf muscles and his perseverance. The top of the tree is where the best fruit is; the rotten fruit drops to the ground. Jennie wanted each girl to recognize that she was worth climbing to the top of the tree for.

A Bozo guy is content with what is on the bottom branches and even what has dropped rotten to the ground, but only a Boaz has the calf muscles—character—to climb to the top of a tree for the best fruit (you).

Psalm 80:12 says, "But now, why have you broken down our walls so that all who pass may steal our fruit?" (NLT). When I read this verse I thought, *You can't steal the fruit high up in a tree as easily as you can the fruit that is hanging on the lowest branches.* Broken walls let trespassers into a garden. If a Bozo guy has broken down one of the walls that guard the fruit of your heart, then allow Jesus to use this book to place some building blocks in your hands that will rebuild where your wall has been broken.

This wall of protection will not keep out an honorable Boaz. In fact, the Man Worth Waiting For has the strength from God not only to climb a tree for you but also to scale a wall to win your heart: "For by You I can run against a troop, by my God I can leap over a wall" (Ps. 18:29 NKJV). Don't settle for a guy who wouldn't leap over a wall for you or climb the highest tree for you! Your heavenly Bridegroom was willing to die for you; don't settle for less in an earthly bridegroom.

On the Same Page

Okay, we've established that Boazes are out there. We've confirmed that finding your Boaz will probably require waiting. But how will you know him when he arrives? Granted, he will have some or most of the qualities we've already talked about. But what is another way to recognize a Boaz?

One day our daughter was wondering the same thing: how would she know which guy was the best for her? I told her that God's best for her would always complement the direction God wanted her to go. In other words, he would have goals similar to hers.

The single life is like a big running track with all these freshly painted lanes. One day she will be running in her lane, relentlessly in pursuit of Jesus, looking ahead and not around, when all of a sudden she will hear this someone approaching.

If this someone is her Boaz, she will not have to stop running, she will not have to change her pace, and she won't have to look behind her, because before she knows it, he will be running alongside her. He will keep up with her, and they will continue the race at a complementary pace. This will be her running partner for the journey ahead. They will encourage each other and not trip each other.

I have met too many women who are running a fabulous race when suddenly they are tripped up by Bozo guys shouting for them to slow down, take a break on the benches with them, and these women are sidetracked for years. Remember to be patient in anticipation of one coming up alongside you, who will also be panting in relentless pursuit of Jesus.

When I was single, I was constantly challenged by the Scripture:

> An unmarried woman or virgin is concerned about the Lord's affairs: Her aim is to be devoted to the Lord in both body and spirit. But a married woman is concerned about the affairs of this world—how she can please her husband. I am saying this for your own good, not to restrict you, but that you may live in a right way in undivided devotion to the Lord. (1 Corinthians 7:34–35)

As a single woman, I could serve the Lord without distraction. But if I got married someday, wouldn't I have to divide my devotion between Jesus and my husband? One day, while I was mulling over this question for the hundredth time, this thought came to me: "Jackie, you will only get married to a man who will enhance your devotion to Me. He will not compete with it."

I got so excited about that answer that I began to pray for a life partner who, along with me, would form a team like the one in Acts named Aquila and Priscilla. In fact, I used to pray that my future mate and I would be a twentieth-century version of this tag team for Jesus.

Author Antoine de Saint-Exupéry wrote, "Life has taught us that love does not consist in gazing at each other, but in looking outward together in the same direction." That was the very thing God showed me about being a tag team for Jesus: my Boaz and I would be on the same page in our devotion to God. When you are considering a guy to date, ask yourself: *Is he looking in the same direction I am?*

For those of us who are followers of Jesus, we know the direction we are to run in and whom to run toward. We know about being careful not to let something or someone hinder our progress in the race. The writer of Hebrews said, "Since we are surrounded by such a great cloud of witnesses [the faithful people listed in Hebrews 11], let us throw off everything that hinders and the sin that so easily entangles, and let us run with perseverance the race marked out for us. Let us fix our eyes on Jesus" (12:1–2).

Notice that this verse emphasizes our need to *throw off* everything that hinders our successfully running the race and staying in our lane. Talk about the need to discard the Bozo you're dating! A Bozo wants you to focus on him, and that requires you to take your eyes off of Jesus—the only One who can help you run the race of life successfully.

Note: Remember that for some, God's best is a lifetime of singleness. One of my college roommates has lived such a life. I have watched her allow God to be enough. Author Nancy DeMoss was asked if she chose singleness. She said, "I chose God's will, and it has been singleness."

Thelma, our movie heroine, was right. You get exactly what

you settle for. A life with a Bozo can lead only to heartache. Settle only for the best instead, whether it's singleness or a relationship with a guy God has designed just for you.

DISCUSSION QUESTIONS

  ❖ Is Boaz a realistic ideal in the twenty-first century? If not, why?

  ❖ Do you think most women settle rather than wait for Boaz? *Isaiah 64:4*

  ❖ How can a woman hang on to her ideals even if she's single year after year? How will you do this, if Boaz takes his time coming?

  ❖ Do you think Louise's comment to Thelma, "You get what you settle for," was harsh or realistic? Why?

  ❖ Describe the top three characteristics of your ideal man. Compare them to the top three that men shared in this chapter.

  ❖ Discuss the illustration of "being on the same page." What does it mean for you?

  ❖ Have you considered whether God might want you to stay single? How do you feel about that? What great single role models do you know?

❀ 3

the counterfeit of a man worth waiting for: bozo

My best friend and I were sitting in the Chicago airport when a young man, talking extremely loud on his cell phone, sat down across from us. He was gushing with loving platitudes to his girlfriend, talking about the great weekend they had together and how much he was going to miss her while he was away. He finished his conversation but not without declaring his undying love several times before saying good-bye.

We were impressed, but only for a moment, because this young man then pulled out a *Hustler* magazine and began checking out all the eye candy. Talk about a Bozo! One minute he was declaring his love to his girlfriend, and then less than a minute later, he was drooling over naked strangers in a magazine. My girlfriend and I were ready to pull out our thumbs and index fingers and make the *Loser* sign. Women need to learn this sign and warn each other when a Bozo is within twenty-five feet.

Do you know how easy it is to find a Bozo? This is how you find a Bozo: close your eyes . . . now open them! Another sure way to find a Bozo is to tap your foot and breathe impatiently when you notice that your watch says, "A quarter past thirty years old." Impatience is a sure escort into the arms of a Bozo.

There is a passage in the New Testament that refers to older women training younger women concerning certain things (Titus 2:4–5). When I examined the Greek word translated "train," I discovered *sophronizo,* which means "call one to her senses (sanity)."[1] I have written this book to call to sanity my precious sisters throughout the world. I am writing to stop the insanity that exists everywhere I travel on this planet. Let's look closely at a Bozo. Are you ready for a sanity checkup?

Bozo Defined

I decided to look up my definition for a Bozo and see if it had changed much since I first published *Lady in Waiting.* In 1995 I described him this way: "A Bozo is a guy whose outward appearance is a façade. It is hard to discern who he really is because of the 'makeup and costume' he wears. What he appears to be physically, socially, and even spiritually is just a performance. A Bozo is a counterfeit of a Boaz—the man worth waiting for."[2]

In *Merriam-Webster's Collegiate Dictionary,* a Bozo is defined as "a foolish or incompetent person," a definition originating in 1916.[3] I wholeheartedly agree with the foolish part, but I have also met many competent men (at least in business) who are absolute Bozos. Now, the incompetent aspect *may* refer to character incompetence, but the dictionary did not clarify that. So I looked at another renowned resource, *The Oxford American College Dictionary*. It defined Bozo as "a stupid, rude, insignificant person, esp. a man."[4] I burst out laughing at Barnes and Noble when I read "esp. a man." This definition was more explicit, and it helped define Bozo beyond a slang expression describing a loser guy. It also gives a definition beyond Bozo the clown, the painted man who is hiding beneath a comical, friendly costume.

We find the biblical example in Amnon, son of King David. You can read the whole story in 2 Samuel 13, but we'll look at it verse by verse here.

Bozos Lust Instead of Love

We read in 2 Samuel 13: "In the course of time, Amnon son of David fell in love with Tamar, the beautiful sister of Absalom son of David" (v. 1).

The verse says, "In the course of time, Amnon . . . *fell in love* with Tamar (italics mine)." Nobody "falls" into love. You don't fall down the stairs into love or trip over a curb into love. No, it's actually falling in lust! Lust means "to look at and set your heart upon."[5] The meaning of the translated "love" in that verse is to "have affection for sexually"![6] Amnon's "affection" was sexual desire. Whenever I hear stories about "love at first sight," I just smile. You can't have love at first sight, but you can have affectionate chemistry at first sight.

Next we read, "Amnon became frustrated to the point of illness on account of his sister Tamar" (v. 2). Have you ever heard people described as being lovesick? That's not a good sign! Getting a little stomachache when you're really excited about someone, that's normal. Amnon was not lovesick, he was lust-sick. Bozos don't know the difference.

Bozos Don't Respect Purity

The passage continues, "Amnon became frustrated to the point of illness on account of his sister Tamar, for she was a virgin and it seemed impossible for him to do anything to her" (v. 2). Princess Tamar's purity was a source of frustration and sickness for Amnon. That is an excellent reflection of the typical Bozo. Bozos do not look in awe upon a woman's purity. Instead of viewing Princess Tamar as a young woman who was beautiful inside and out, Amnon was actually full of angst because of her virginity and his lack of opportunity to do anything to her. Her unconquered virginity made this Bozo ill!

Right there we have a loser in 3-D. A Bozo is not attracted to purity. In fact, all he wants to do is conquer and rob girls of purity. Talk about a predator! Do you feel an urge to make the *Loser* symbol right now? Unfortunately this story gets worse, and you will have many more opportunities to use that symbol.

Bozos Measure a Woman by Externals

In these verses we see that Prince Bozo was attracted by Princess Tamar's beauty. Something to ponder: Bozos always define a woman externally. They're obsessed with what's outside a woman. When they describe women young or old, they always focus on looks. They never use terms like *nice, sweet, kind, thoughtful, compassionate, friendly, outgoing*—Bozos don't know anything about internal character qualities. They think "internal qualities" refers to guts. The American obsession with body beautiful is not fueled by Men Worth Waiting For, but, sadly, by the ever-increasing Bozo Tribe!

Bozos Keep Bad Company

Second Samuel continues:

> Now Amnon had a friend named Jonadab son of Shimeah, David's brother. Jonadab was a very shrewd man. He asked Amnon, "Why do you, the king's son, look so haggard morning after morning? Won't you tell me?"
>
> Amnon said to him, "I am in love with Tamar, my brother Absalom's sister."
>
> "Go to bed and pretend to be ill," Jonadab said. "When your father comes to see you, say to him, 'I would like my sister Tamar to come and give me something to eat. Let her prepare the food in my sight so I may watch her and then eat it from her hand.' " (vv. 3–5)

All Bozos have fans and cheerleaders. We will discuss the cheerleaders in another chapter, but right now we will look at the zealous fan who cheered on this Bozo prince. Jonadab asked, "Why do you, the king's son, look so haggard morning after morning?" In other words, "What are you so upset about?"

Fans of Bozos do not think that looking haggard is a tolerable condition. A Bozo fan wants to see the clown smiling perpetually, believing the Bozo is entitled to perpetual joy and pleasure. Jonadab's remark also enforces Amnon's entitlement mentality: "You are the son of a king. You deserve only happiness!"

"Haggard" refers to looking worn-out—Amnon was worn-out by his lust for Princess Tamar. He wasn't energized by honorable love but was drained by destructive lust. In the original language of this verse, the expression is: "Why are you, the king's son, just dangling in need from dawn to dusk?"[7] Is that not a powerful expression—"dangling in need" from the rope of lust? Yikes!

Amnon said, "I'm so in love with Tamar, but there's just no way to get her alone, because she's a virgin." His friend replied, "I've got an idea!" Now this is the kind of friend that you hope the guy you admire does not have as a steady influence in his life. A man will reflect the men he spends most of his time with.

Jonadab came up with a plan on how to get the two of them alone: "Fake being sick. Ask your dad to send for Princess Tamar, to let her come cook for you, so you guys can be alone."

Bozos Are Dangerous

Notice that Jonadab suggested Princess Tamar come and cook for Prince Bozo so he can "watch her" prepare the meal. This is not an opportunity for some admirable attention but for a predator's premeal drooling!

It is worth noting that Cousin Jonadab was not only a cheerleader for Amnon's impurity, later he even shared responsibility for Amnon's death (2 Sam. 13:30–39). Jonadab cheered on the lust that ultimately led to Amnon's death. Where are the courageous friends who cheer men on to moral purity?

Bozos keep poor company who encourage their baser instincts.

Bozos' Talk Doesn't Match Their Walk

Amnon's name meant "trustworthy."[8] A Bozo is a man who does not live his name. Amnon's actions were the opposite of trustworthy. This includes Christian guys who do not act like Christians (people belonging to Christ). I don't care if you tell me he says he's a Christian; let him prove it by the way he lives. A lot of people use the name Christian, but they don't live as if it's true. When I say to people, "I'm a follower of Jesus," or "I'm white-hot, madly in love with Jesus," I back it up with how I live my life.

> God has driven the ideal qualities of manhood deep into my heart by showing me men who showed less-than-ideal qualities as well as the stellar ones.
>
> —George Toles, marketing expert and former NBA broadcaster

Amnon was also a prince, a "son of David." He didn't live up to that title either.

Bozos Are Deceptive

We read further in 2 Samuel 13:

> So Amnon lay down and pretended to be ill. When the king came to see him, Amnon said, "I would like my sister Tamar to come and make some special bread in my sight, so I may eat from her hand."
>
> David sent word to Tamar at the palace: "Go to the house of your brother Amnon, and prepare some food for him." So Tamar went to the house of her brother Amnon, who was lying down. She took some dough,

> In my opinion, an ideal godly man should embody three things: faithfulness to God and family, man of His Word, love for others.
>
> —*Steve, pharmacist*

kneaded it, made the bread in his sight and baked it. Then she took the pan and served him the bread, but he refused to eat. "Send everyone out of here," Amnon said. So everyone left him. (vv. 6–9)

Amnon said to his dad, King David, "I'm not feeling good. Could you send Tamar in to cook for me?" King David was not discerning enough to ask his son why he needed Tamar to cook for him when he already had a full staff waiting on his every whim. Why was his father so oblivious? The adultery in David's own life (2 Sam. 11–12) gave him a blind spot regarding his lust-driven Bozo son. So, an adulterous father helped a fornicating son set the stage for the conquering of Princess Tamar's virginity.

Fathers so often pass their own blind spots to their sons as a living legacy that will choke them with the same obsession. One time I heard a father say to his eight-year-old son who was watching a movie, "Hey buddy, isn't that babe hot?" Talk about a Bozo Training Moment. This father was a very intelligent, successful businessman, but he had reverted to the American lie that true masculinity parallels sexual prowess.

Bozos lie—especially to get what they want.

Bozos Exploit Women

When Princess Tamar received word that the king wanted her to go cook for her half-brother Amnon, I wonder why she didn't ask, *Why does Amnon need me to cook for him, since he has a full staff?* Maybe she did ask but no one answered—no one would have questioned a king's command.

Princess Tamar went to cook for Prince Bozo. Her walking into a secluded situation with a Bozo was the very environment for her exploitation. Daily, women stroll casually into private places with men who do not have the purest of motives.

Unfortunately, the things I imitate from my father are the negative things.

—Eddie Taubensee, retired baseball player and ambassador for Major League Baseball in Pro Athletes Outreach

"Then she took the pan and served him the bread, but he refused to eat. 'Send everyone out of here,' Amnon said. So everyone left him" (v. 9). Princess Tamar was cooking, and all of a sudden Prince Bozo commanded all the staff to get out. "Tell everybody to go away!" Right then a security signal should have gone off in Princess Tamar's head! Amnon did not want to be alone with Princess Tamar so he could talk heart to heart. He didn't want to be alone so they could give each other pedicures! Guys do not want to be alone with girls so they can watch the latest chick flick.

When I speak to girls about guys wanting to be alone with them, I warn them that a guy's motives are rarely pure. When a guy says he wants to come over and study for the English final, often his real motive is to come over and study his favorite subject, female geography! You may be thinking that you are mature enough to spend a lot of time alone with a guy without becoming involved sexually. Well, that may be true if the guy is someone you are not at all attracted to, but that is the exception. Men by nature are not very verbal, and after so much talking, they are ready for *sports*—either *SportsCenter* on TV or sports with your body!

Please hear me clearly: The main reason guys want to be alone with girls is not because they're in the presence of such intelligence and they just want to hear them talk! No, they want the girls to stop talking! They are not interested in exploring women's souls; they are more interested in exploring women's bodies. Bozos always want you alone because being alone always leads to new exploitation and experimentation! Understand that when a guy wants to be with just you, it isn't because he wants to say something to you that is so intimate it is only for your ears. He wants to be intimate, but not verbally.

When I was a junior in high school, I had a crush on a man I worked with at a military commissary. What I didn't know was that he was married. He flirted with me incessantly, and finally, one day during a lunch break, we went out to his car and started making out, hot and heavy. A day later, I found out he was married, and I was devastated. This Bozo took advantage of a girl's love-hungry heart. How pathetic, but how typical when it comes to the exploitation that is second nature for a Bozo.

Just for a moment, let's look at this on an adolescent level. When teens are first alone, they hold hands and get the thrill of the century! Then the next time they're alone, they hold hands again. This time they wonder, *Is that the same hand? I held that hand last Friday night and it was much more thrilling then. How come I'm holding it this Friday night, and it's not as big a deal?* Touch is almost like cocaine! People snort one line of cocaine, and the next time they try it, it's not as satisfying. They have to do more and more and more! This is called the law of diminishing returns, and I am amazed how few adults even give it a moment's consideration.

Yet, on an adult level, the progression is even faster sexually, because adults think they are so liberated and sophisticated that moral guidelines are for irresponsible teens, not consenting, informed adults.

Suffice it to say for now, Bozos who want alone time usually want more than your ear.

Bozos Disregard Consequences

> But when she took it to him to eat, he grabbed her and said, "Come to bed with me, my sister."
>
> "Don't, my brother!" she said to him. "Don't force me.... Don't do this wicked thing. What about me? Where could I get rid of my disgrace? What about you? You would be like one of the wicked fools in Israel. Please speak to the king; he will not keep me from being married to you." (vv. 11–13)

There in that moment of terror, Tamar had the common sense to remind her half-brother of who he was and what he was risking by attacking her. But Bozos don't care about consequences.

Bozos Don't Listen

Tamar said, "Don't do this, please don't do what I think you're getting ready to do. Please!" She was pleading, but she wasn't heard. That's how you know you're in the presence of a Bozo: he can never hear you! All he hears is the beat of his own lustful heart: "But he refused to listen to her, and since he was stronger than she, he raped her" (v. 14).

Notice Princess Tamar said, "Don't do this wicked thing.

What about me? Where could I get rid of my disgrace?" That is the saddest remark, and women have repeated it throughout the ages. Every time a man exploits a woman sexually, he disregards how she feels in order to follow his lust. Prince Amnon could not hear Tamar's plea because his ears were clogged by entitlement. Just think of the millions of women who have said to the guys they were with, "I don't think we should go any further." Yet the guys managed to persuade them—not necessarily physically as Amnon did Tamar, but I believe that daily, women are raped emotionally and seduced into sexual sin against their better judgment. Daily, women submit to a Bozo's pleading voice, hoping to secure love, only to end up with disgrace and self-hatred. Remember: men play at love to get sex and women play at sex to get love.

Bozos Are Fools Caught in Folly

"Don't do it because you'll be like one of the fools of Israel," Tamar pleaded. I looked up that term—"fools of Israel." It means "stupidly wicked."[9] Proverbs says, "It is safer to meet a bear robbed of her cubs than to confront a fool caught in folly" (17:12 NLT). So Tamar found out.

You may be thinking, *I would never go out with such a Bozo. I wouldn't even talk on the phone with someone like that!* The problem is that Bozos don't appear to be Bozos initially. They appear to be charming and adorable. But they're playing with your heart to see how much they can exploit you. Bozos are bent on their own way. A princess can plead and scream and say no, but a Bozo—even a Prince Bozo—doesn't listen.

Before we finish this story, I need to address an issue: how many young girls are impressed when older boys pay attention to them. It shocks me how giddy girls get when an older guy says something nice to them at school. I want to ask, "Where's your mother? What's your address? Where do you live? I'm coming to your house tonight. I'll call your mother! I'm telling on you!" I mean, I'd be every child's nightmare if I could.

An older boy likes a younger girl for one reason: he knows he can get his way more effectively because she's so in awe of him!

What she doesn't understand is the reason he doesn't date girls his own age: he has already used those girls and broken their hearts, so he has to move on to younger victims. When older guys look your way, don't be impressed. Bozos are committed to folly, and they want to engage in it with you!

Bozos Expect You to Prove Your Love

At the beginning of this story the Scripture says, "In the course of time, Amnon . . . fell in love with Tamar." Then, when he got his desires satisfied sexually—was he *then more in love with her*?

Precious girls, hear me now: when you go too far with a guy physically, you do it hoping that he's going to love you even more! Even in your heart you're saying, *We shouldn't be doing this, we shouldn't be doing this . . . my dad would kill you if he knew we were doing this!* But you go on, because you want so much for this guy to love you.

Listen to what the Scripture says. Amnon supposedly *loved* Tamar. Now jump ahead to 2 Samuel 13:15. When he got done with her physically, it says, "Then Amnon hated her with intense hatred. In fact, he hated her more than he had loved her." How do you figure that? Wait a minute—if you let a guy have his way, he should be worshiping you, lighting candles and burning incense in front of your picture! But no. Bozos use and then move on! They use and then dispose of you like a Kleenex they blew their noses in.

Don't compromise. Don't give guys more than what you know in your heart is right! Don't do it! So many women are doing it because they think they're going to earn their guys' love.

Now why did Amnon hate Tamar so intensely? Because his conscience started to bother him. When boys who are raised in Christian homes go too far with girls who are raised in Christian homes, their consciences (usually) really start to protest. The boys feel guilt, and they start blaming the girls. If you are a Christian (in the true sense of the word), then you are a princess, and you will feel guilt when you violate God's moral code. Amnon, who knew better, raped his half-sister. Then he resented her for the guilt he felt.

The first Christian guy I dated was on staff in a teen ministry, and we had the greatest relationship. Everyone thought we were the ideal couple. I was thrilled to be dating a Boaz and not a Bozo. Well, one night after a very dramatic event, we were kissing and we went too far . . . not far by today's standards, but far by our standards. In less than a week, he broke up with me. I didn't understand, and I was absolutely devastated. But years later, when studying this passage, I realized that my Boaz went farther than his heavenly King would have wanted him to, and his guilt caused his love for me to turn to repulsion.

I want you to know that when I first read this story about Amnon and Tamar, I had an absolute fit in my dorm room! I was stunned for days. I probably shared this passage with anyone I got within two feet of. It's such an explicit and true-to-life example—even in the twenty-first century—of a man with a

Bozo nature and the harm he could do to a defenseless woman. You, however, can be a wise woman who knows how to defend herself against Bozos and seek instead the gentle Boazes who will protect, not harm you.

DISCUSSION QUESTIONS

- ✿ Have you known or dated many Bozos? Share an illustration of a Bozo in your life.
- ✿ Discuss the classic example of a Bozo—Prince Amnon. What was Amnon's motivation? What does this story say to you about the influence of a scheming friend like Jonadab?
- ✿ Consider and discuss the transforming power of guilt that can turn love into hate after lust is gratified. *2 Samuel 13:1–2, 15* Have you seen this happen?
- ✿ An experience with a Bozo can be a beneficial tutorial when a woman:
    1. Dissects the experience.
    2. Discerns characteristics (both his and hers) that led to the bad experience.
    3. Determines to change hers; learns how to recognize his.
    4. Releases regret.

    Discuss an experience with a Bozo in which you were able eventually to dissect, discern, determine, and release.

part II

the essential elements of a MWWF

From the beginning of time, the Creator designed man to exhibit certain qualities, not as an exceptional achievement, but as a true reflection of his Creator. As a creation of God, Boaz demonstrated these characteristics. We'll look at these in the next few chapters. Note: No man will demonstrate all of these qualities perfectly or all of the time. But a truly godly man—a Man Worth Waiting For—will display patterns in his life that reflect a heart's passion for the ways and will of God. As one of my survey respondents, Sue, wrote, "Ultimately, an ideal man knows who he is and who he was created to be." You'll see this in the MWWF God brings your way.

✿ 4

farmers and princes

Whom would you choose to date—a prince or a farmer? This question may seem absurd, considering the obvious contrast between the two. The main character in the last chapter was a prince of Israel, but if a single girl had chosen him over the farmer we will be looking at in this chapter, her choice would have been disastrous.

This question is not about the innate value of either a farmer or a prince, but rather the superficial conclusion many women make in relation to Mr. Right. We assume that a woman would choose a prince before she would choose a farmer. She would choose Joe Millionaire over a hardworking guy in overalls.

Just recently, I read an article about a modern Prince Charming, though he didn't sound as attractive as one would expect. He was middle-aged, balding, and paunchy, yet he never lacked female attention. This modern Prince Charming sounded more to me like the stereotypical farmer. So what could be the attraction? This particular description of a most eligible bachelor was of the Prince of Monaco—Prince Albert.

The story reminded me of a trend that is so prevalent and so sad. Why would so many women be attracted to such an ordinary man? Although he *is* charming, wouldn't the balding head and paunchy stomach leave something to be desired? So why does he secure so much attention all over the world? Simply because his title is Prince, and his supposed net worth is two billion dollars. And that's enough to change a frog into a prince—or a Bozo into a Boaz—in the eyes of plenty of women.

A very successful hairstylist verified this, telling me that over the years he has seen the saddest thing in the lives of most of his clients: "Women no longer marry for love, because they don't believe true love exists. They assume it is an extinct reality. Instead of love, women now marry for money and power."

Why will a woman keep dating a man who has not been honest with her? Why will she continue to hang on to the relationship when it has already died emotionally? Why does a woman stay married to an unfaithful husband? Why does a woman remain in a relationship that all her friends and family see is destructive? Too often it is because she has said yes to the prince rather than the farmer. She has a vested interest in the illusion of security that money and power promise her. She doesn't think the ideal man exists, whether he is a farmer or a day trader.

In the last chapter we saw that Amnon was a prince—whom many women would have chosen over the man we are going to look at more closely in this chapter: Farmer Boaz. And we will look at the essential qualities he exhibited—and that your MWWF will exhibit today.

A MWWF Has Noble Character

Boaz's name means "in him is strength" or "pillar of strength."[1] One of the pillars at the entrance of the temple in Jerusalem was called Boaz. As you study the brief yet important love story of Ruth, you discover that this quality of strength is reflected in the principled man that Boaz was.

In the second chapter of Ruth, the first statement made about this Man Worth Waiting For is this: "Now Naomi had a relative of her husband's, a worthy man of the clan of Elimelech, whose name was Boaz" (Ruth 2:1 ESV).

"Worthy" refers to a man of noble character. While Boaz was clearly a wealthy, eligible bachelor, the prominence he achieved through power and money was not his only asset. He was a man of strong character. Many a man can achieve prominence through financial prowess, but money cannot purchase what is lasting in value—godly character.

A Noble Man Loves in Action as Well as Words

This year I saw another example of a man with noble character in the remake of *Pride and Prejudice*. The leading man, Mr. Darcy, ended up winning the heart of the leading woman, Elizabeth, because he lived the principles of strength. Mr. Darcy did some very noble things to preserve the honor of the family of the woman he loved. And even after all he did for her, in the last scene of the movie he was willing to let her go if she wasn't

> An ideal man is trustworthy and wise and maintains a quiet strength.
> —Kimberly Richens, teacher

willing to be his journey partner. In fact, he said, "You are too generous to travel with me."

This humble remark caused me to reflect on the similarities between Boaz and Mr. Darcy. As he declared his love for Elizabeth at the end of the movie, Mr. Darcy said, "You must know that everything I did, I did for you." His love for Elizabeth was not in *word only but in deed* (1 John 3:18)—an important trademark of a good man.

Mr. Darcy served Elizabeth before he even was assured of winning her heart. In the same way, Boaz served Ruth by protecting her and providing for her—even before she suggested he be her kinsman-redeemer.

Mr. Darcy and Boaz served the women they loved—even when the assurance of these women as future journey partners was not secure. The noble deeds Mr. Darcy and Boaz undertook to win the hearts of the women they loved were not exceptional but very typical of Men Worth Waiting For.

A Noble Man Inspires Respect

Boaz arrived at his fields to check on the harvest. He greeted the harvesters by saying, "The LORD be with you" (Ruth 2:4). Now, that is not a superficial greeting like our common hello or "How ya doin'?" Reflected in that comment was a noble man's longing for God to bless his employees. Is that not great? Here was a boss concerned about his employees' being blessed. In *The Heritage Bible*, this verse reads: "And behold, Boaz came from Bethlehem, and said to the reapers, Jehovah be with you.

And they answered him, Jehovah kneel down with goodness to you."[2]

Read that phrase closely: "Jehovah kneel down with goodness." Employees wanted God to stoop down and bless their wonderful master/employer. Boaz lived the principle penned by another Hebrew single guy named Paul, who would write centuries later: "Masters, supply your slaves [another word: employees] with what is right and fair, because you know that you also have a Master in heaven" (Col. 4:1).

The respect between Boaz and his workers is a sharp contrast to the relationship between another wealthy Hebrew and his employees: Nabal. Nabal means "fool" in Hebrew.[3] Listen to what one of his employees said about him: "He's so ill-tempered that no one can even talk to him!" (1 Sam. 25:17 NLT).

Notice how the various single men you know greet one another. Think about the depth or the superficiality of their encounters. The single apostle Paul wrote, "Let your speech always be gracious, seasoned with salt, so that you may know how you should answer each person" (Col. 4:6 ESV). Every greeting does not have to contain profound theological content, but consider the potential depth a greeting can have when two good guys (or girls) meet in the workplace, a church hallway, or even the dry cleaner's.

Do the single men you know stick to superficialities, or do they use greetings to bless others? A Boaz would open a conversation with something besides sport statistics or the stock price index of Microsoft.

A man of noble character knows how to love long-term. How important is character? That can be answered with another question: how important is love? Love that lasts beyond the seven-year itch, love that lasts beyond financial setbacks, love for better or for worse is love that is supported by depth of character.

Love is a choice, not just a feeling. Emotions come and go, but a choice is reinforced by one's character. The problem today with many men is a lack of real character development. Bozos love when they feel like it. Boazes love enduringly. The growth of character enhances a man's capacity to love well and long-term.

The commitment phobia that so many use as an excuse for singleness is a reflection of shallow character. Character and love are inextricably linked, as noted by author C. S. Lewis in *Mere Christianity*: "Love, as distinct from being in love, is not merely a feeling. It is a deep unity, maintained by the will and deliberately strengthened by habit; reinforced by [in Christian marriages] the grace which both partners ask, and receive, from God."

A man's character is revealed during times of trial. On a date in a controlled environment, a guy can appear to be a Boaz. But it is critical to have an opportunity to see how he responds to stress and disappointment because his response reveals his character. Moses wrote: "Remember how the LORD your God led you through the wilderness for forty years, humbling you and testing you to prove your character, and to find out whether or not you would really obey his commands" (Deut. 8:2 NLT).

When you're considering a guy's character, trying to discern if he is a Boaz or a Bozo, ask yourself: *Is this person qualified to help me obey God?* Another way to phrase it: *Does this guy draw me closer to God or distract me from God?*

A Boaz will encourage you to obey God.

A Bozo will encourage you to disobey God.

He who loves you most will help you obey God! My husband and I taught a large singles' Bible study for five years. We challenged more than a hundred singles every week with this exhortation from Hebrews: "And let us consider how we may spur one another on toward love and good deeds" (Heb. 10:24). Are you looking for a man who will encourage you to obey God, or have you been spending time with a man who encourages you to disregard what God is showing you?

> An ideal godly man should be faithful, a man . . . who follows through when he says he is going to do something. Perhaps this is so important to me because of the lack of consistency I have experienced with men. . . . People very easily throw around words.
> —Ana C. Cerrato, finance manager

A Noble Man Exhibits the "Three I's"

The "Three I's" are *identity in Christ, integrity in life*, and *initiative*. I heard that guys on one seminary campus wrote the "Three I's" on their hands. That may seem silly to you, but for a man who desires to know who he is in Jesus, to live a life framed by integrity, and to operate from the initiative of God's dream for him, the "Three I's" are a wonderful reminder.

Apparently the "Three I's" were once taught in a course called Godly Manhood, but unfortunately this class has been dropped from the curriculum. Once again, this reminds me that universities across America pack the curriculum with courses to breed intelligent graduates, yet I meet thousands of people who continue to pass school and flunk life. Yes, men do this too!

Make sure the guy you invest your heart in has strong, godly principles. Otherwise he's a Bozo, and he's not worth your time.

A MWWF Protects

We've seen that noble character marks a man of God—a Man Worth Waiting For. Now we'll look at another nonnegotiable quality in a Boaz: he protects women. A MWWF senses that many men seek to exploit women, especially the vulnerable ones. Boaz was quick to protect Ruth, not only physically, but also emotionally. Let's jump back into the story and see how.

Boaz Provides Physical Protection

When Boaz arrived from Bethlehem, he asked his laborers, "Whose young woman is that?" The job foreman said, "That's Ruth, she's the Moabitess who came back with Naomi." When he said "She's the Moabitess," he was saying, "She's that foreigner from the wrong side of the tracks."

Did that inference distract Boaz? No! The protector in Boaz kicked into gear. He called Ruth over and said, "Don't go and glean in another field and don't go away from here. Stay here with my servant girls. Watch the field where the men are harvesting, and follow along after the girls. I have told the men not to touch you" (Ruth 2:8–9). He encouraged her to stay in his field of safety.

You may wonder, *Why would men touch her if she's harvesting? What does harvesting have to do with guys getting out of hand?* In those days, when a woman came and filled her apron full of barley or wheat, laborers would sort of heckle her as she left the field: "Hey, you got a lot of free wheat there!" meaning, "How about a little something in return?" I read that it was not unusual for a foreigner to be raped after she had gathered free grain. Note: men who think women owe them for a handout are typical Bozos.

As I've mentioned, the free grain Ruth gathered was a promise of the Law of God. It was God's gracious welfare system for the needy. Ruth was gathering what God had designated as her rightful share—no payment necessary but a heart of gratitude.

Boaz knew that some men took advantage of the needy women who gleaned in the fields. That's why he warned his men not to touch Ruth. What is so precious is that Boaz warned the men before he called Ruth over. When he spoke to her, he had already acted to protect her sexually.

Recently a baseball coach said to me, "Jackie, all men are capable of acting inappropriately towards women—whether in sexual harassment, crude remarks, or worse." Boaz wanted to protect Ruth sexually. What a contrast to the Bozo, who would exploit needy and vulnerable women.

Let's look at a modern example of this exploitation. It makes me insane when a girl thinks that she owes a man more than a "thank you" at the end of a date. What do you do after being taken to a nice place to eat and maybe to a good movie? When he walks you up to the door, you say, "Thank you." You don't owe him a "thank you" with your body. This guy just had the privilege of spending an evening with you. The gift of your presence and your gratitude for his generosity are plenty. And if that ain't enough, he's a Bozo!

Just because your date got tickets to the hottest show on Broadway or the concert of the decade doesn't mean you owe him a hot time in the sack at the end of the date. When a woman "pays" a man with sexual favors, she is acting like a prostitute. Do single girls ultimately prostitute themselves in the hope of securing a lasting love? Sometimes they do. You know it and I know it.

Ruth, having come from the degenerate nation of Moab, was especially vulnerable. Too often men will take advantage of a woman's less-than-perfect background. They reason, *She's used to rough treatment. Why not give her what she's used to?* Bozos seem to be able to sniff out the most defenseless women.

This terrible danger of women being taken advantage of at the workplace (wow, sexual harassment even then!) was something Ruth's mother-in-law, Naomi, addressed: "It will be good for you, my daughter, to go with his girls, because in someone else's field you might be harmed" (Ruth 2:22). Naomi knew that her daughter-in-law might be treated inappropriately even while she worked to get food. It is so sad that a single girl would be harassed while doing something so noble: working hard to take care of herself and her family.

Boaz Provides Emotional Protection

Boaz not only protected Ruth physically, he instructed his male laborers in a way that protected her emotionally. Boaz said to his men, "Even if she gathers among the sheaves, don't embarrass her" (Ruth 2:15). Boaz knew that the Law allowed Ruth to pick up the leftovers, the gleanings, but she was only to glean in specific areas. Boaz was concerned that one of the guys would say, "You're in the wrong spot, babe!"

Bozo men talk like that; they make you feel two feet tall. When Boaz told his men not to embarrass Ruth, he gave them a command, not a suggestion: "Boaz gave orders to his men" (Ruth 2:15). He not only ordered the men to not embarrass Ruth, he also commanded them to leave a little extra grain for her to gather.

I have watched more guys embarrass girls at school, work, or social gatherings. These guys say things that totally humiliate the young women who are with them. The next time you witness a guy embarrassing his date or a girl who is a friend, pray for the courage to confront the girl about her relationship with such a Bozo. When I see a man publicly humiliate a woman, I immediately think, *Another Bozo has been unleashed on the world.*

I think we should have Bozo prisons. All the Bozos get parole only when they have seen the total error of their Bozo bent. They can be released only when their rehabilitation leads to an intentional attitude of living like a modern Boaz. When they are transformed, they will want to protect women in their purity and help protect their hearts.

Sad to say, Christian girls today don't expect to be treated with honor. They don't expect guys to be in awe of them. They're so in awe of the guys, they'll do whatever the guys want! A normal, proper attitude toward you as a young woman is one of respect and protection. Men should protect your honor and your purity. A Boaz does.

You know what makes me sad? You know why we have to sign purity pledges? We have to hold the standard up, because guys don't respect us enough to say, "Oh sweetheart, your life is so pure, I wouldn't touch you!" One time a guy said to me, "You know, there's something about your daughter. You just respect her and want to honor her." I thought, *How can we get that for other girls? Can we package that and sell it?* Boaz wanted to protect Ruth through respect and honor.

Where do you think Boaz got his sensitivity training? Consider his background. He was raised by a mom who knew firsthand how men can take advantage of women! Did you know that Boaz's mom was Rahab the harlot? Boaz was raised by a woman with a colorful past, but her wise choices decided her future destiny. Rahab chose the God of Israel, she rescued Israel's spies (who later saved her life), and she raised a boy who became a principled protector of women (Josh. 2). Rahab trained her son to understand: guys are here to protect, not exploit, women.

If Boaz hasn't impressed you yet, keep reading. I hope that reading this book will help detox you from your overexposure to Bozo guys and your deprivation of hope in relation to the Man Worth Waiting For. Such a man does exist. I know, I married one, and I know one who has been raised in our household. And besides those two, my daughter married such a man, and I could introduce you to many others that I know across the U.S.!

A MWWF Provides

A third essential quality is that of being a provider. As I remember my first love, I am embarrassed to admit that he was a total Bozo. If I wanted *anything* to happen in our relationship financially, I had to come up with the funds!

When I wanted to attend a special social event that required a corsage, I had to buy my own. When I wanted to go to my favorite dance event, I not only had to pay for both of us, I had to arrange the ride. My first love invested all his funds in his number-one love—and it wasn't me. His number-one love was surfing, and he used every dime he had to compete in surfing contests and to repair his surfboard daily!

Most likely you are thinking, *Typical adolescent behavior!* And it may be true that such behavior can be overlooked in adolescence, but I have met far too many women paying too much financially (and emotionally) for their relationships. A girl who wasn't provided for in her teens can't expect any different when she's a woman—if she stays with the same man.

Researchers do many studies on women's needs, and constantly surfacing as one of the top five is financial security. Boaz's provision for Ruth was not just a flirting gesture. It was meeting a poor foreigner's deep need—it was caring for a young widow who was trying to provide not only for herself but for her widowed mother-in-law. Boaz's provision for these women reflected his respect for the Law: "[God] shows love to the foreigners living among you and gives them food and clothing. You, too, must show love to foreigners, for you yourselves were once foreigners in the land of Egypt" (Deut. 10:18–19 NLT).

Notice that Boaz provided Ruth with more than she even needed. Let's look at the passage:

> At mealtime Boaz said to her, "Come over here. Have some bread and dip it in the wine vinegar."
>
> When she sat down with the harvesters, he offered her some roasted grain. She ate all she wanted and had some left over. As she got up to glean, Boaz gave orders to his men, "Even if she gathers among the sheaves, don't embarrass her. Rather, pull out some stalks for her from the bundles and leave them for her to pick up, and don't rebuke her." (Ruth 2:14–16)

> An ideal man is generous, not only to me personally, but in general: [to] God's work, God's people, and the needy.
>
> —Ana C. Cerrato, finance manager

After sharing lunch with her, Boaz even secretly arranged for greater provision! He was quite extravagant. As I previously noted, he went beyond what the Hebrew Law required for the needy. The Hebrew Law required only that Boaz give Ruth the leftovers of his harvest—but he gave from the harvest itself.

Why does a woman settle for a man who is too self-absorbed to give her more than she needs? Why do women so willingly settle for crumbs? Why do so many bright, wonderful girls act like the needy teen I was in high school, always paying for the privilege of being loved? Do women so want male attention that they are willing to pay for it rather than be the recipient of blessings initiated in secret, like Boaz's provision for Ruth?

When you're sorting the Boazes from the Bozos in life, look at how the man gives. Does he give freely, generously, offer more than enough? Or does he cling to his wallet, dispersing funds reluctantly or morosely? A Boaz gladly provides.

Resting Under the Same Set of Wings

The psalmist wrote:

> *Those who live in the shelter of the Most High*
> *will find rest in the shadow of the Almighty.*
> *This I declare about the LORD:*
> *He alone is my refuge, my place of safety;*

he is my God, and I trust him. . . .
He will cover you with his feathers.
  He will shelter you with his wings.
  His faithful promises are your armor and protection.

                          (Psalm 91:1–2, 4 NLT)

During the first conversation between Boaz and Ruth, Boaz made a reference to Ruth's resting under God's wings. That may sound like a lovely poetic phrase, but it was a serious place of security for the one who was trusting in God alone. Boaz said, "May the LORD, the God of Israel, under whose wings you have come to take refuge, reward you fully" (Ruth 2:12 NLT). This remark was more than a charming response; it was a perceptive observation of the condition of Ruth's spiritual life.

Boaz was keenly aware of the faith that was required of Ruth to leave her family, country, and gods, travel with Naomi back to her hometown and country, and choose to trust in the God of Israel. We can see in this part of the conversation between Boaz and Ruth that these two singles were trusting in the God of Israel to provide their needs—body, soul, and spirit. Both of them had found shelter in the shadow of God's wings.

Before Ruth met this noble, protective provider, her mother-in-law expressed the prayer of her heart: "May the LORD bless you with the security of another marriage" (Ruth 1:9 NLT). How ironic that one of Boaz's original remarks to Ruth is acknowledging that she had discovered a secure place under the wings of God. Ruth was ready to rest under Boaz's wings *only when she had first discovered her eternal security underneath the wings of Almighty God.* Ruth found a safe place under the wings of a man who himself lived securely under the wings of the Almighty.

A Bozo offers no security because he holds back financially and emotionally. A Boaz provides joyfully. Don't settle for anything but the best!

A MWWF Is a Persistent Pursuer

The fourth quality has to do with a man's energies for the people he cares for. Naomi recognized Boaz's honorable qualities. She felt sure his intentions were pure and that he was worthy of her daughter-in-law. She saw that Boaz was a man of good character who was eager to follow God's Law. After Ruth had asked Boaz to be her kinsman-redeemer, Naomi said: "Wait, my daughter, until you find out what happens. For the man *will not rest* until the matter is settled today" (Ruth 3:18, italics mine).

Notice this characteristic at work: Boaz approached Ruth first. He instigated their relationship. When she responded, he was persistent in his pursuit.

When Ruth asked Boaz if he could be her kinsman-redeemer, not only was Boaz's response compassionate, but it also showed that a man of noble character was drawn to a woman of the same character. A woman attracts her heart's companion. As we've seen, Boaz's reply to Ruth's request for the need of a kinsman-redeemer was this: "And now, my daughter, don't be afraid. I will do for you all you ask. All my fellow townsmen know that you are a woman of noble character" (Ruth 3:11).

Boaz made a promise to Ruth, and he was persistent in discovering whether he qualified as the nearest kinsman to redeem all the land that had belonged to Naomi's and Ruth's husbands.

Such honorable pursuit and persistence stand in such contrast to the training that men today receive in relation to being a MWWF. From a young age, men are trained how to hide their feelings, how to win in a fistfight, how to hit a ball, how to shoot a gun, how to birdie on the sixteenth hole, and how to manipulate several remote controls simultaneously. Some men live a whole lifetime and never master the science of How to Handle a Woman. The apostle Peter had a wife, and he knew from firsthand experience what he wrote about in 1 Peter 3:7: "Husbands, dwell with [your wives] according to knowledge" (KJV). The word translated "knowledge" comes from a Greek word meaning "science."[4] A woman is a science to be studied and discovered, but so few men are coached or mentored into loving women as they need to be loved. We see in Ephesians that Paul's great commandment to men is to love them as much as Christ loves the church (Eph. 5:25). Talk about a sacrificial love!

A Bozo will love a woman in whatever way he feels is best— in whatever way serves him, not her. A Boaz will love a woman in a way that *shows* his feelings—and persistence in meeting a woman's needs is one way he does this.

A MWWF Is a Prepared Partner

Such a great social distance existed between Boaz, a man of standing, and Ruth the Moabitess, that his protection and provision were stunning gestures to this girl from the lower end of the social yardstick. Ruth acknowledged this in her response: "At this, she bowed down with her face to the ground. She exclaimed, 'Why have I found such favor in your eyes that you notice me—a foreigner?'" (Ruth 2:10).

Why *did* Boaz respond with such honor rather than dishonor toward the Moabitess Ruth? A distinctive aspect of Boaz is that he was a *prepared partner*. He was attuned to the heart and needs of the woman in his life. Consider the sensitivity that permeated the heart of Boaz's mother. Rahab was not only gracious herself to foreigners, we can assume she taught her son the same quality.

A prepared partner is always ready and willing to attend to another's needs. We've seen that Boaz was responsive to Ruth's vulnerability both emotionally and physically. A Boaz expresses and acts on his compassion for others. A Bozo, on the other hand, focuses on himself. He may briefly pity someone in his life, but he doesn't actually do much to help her.

Let me tell you about a modern-day Boaz and how he showed this quality of being attuned to his Ruth.

When my daughter was about to be married, the groom's mother and I were invited to attend Jessi's bachelorette party. After dinner and a chick flick, we traveled back to the home of the matron of honor, Sandy. There Sandy played a video of Drew's taped responses to questions he'd been asked the night before. After each question, Sandy stopped the tape so Jessi could give her answers. Then Sandy played the video to see how close Drew came to the right response.

It was so impressive because Drew got every question exactly right! As the questions continued, everyone in the room became overwhelmed with the amount of detail that Drew knew about Jessi. The girls all began to say, "We want someone who knows our hearts the way Drew knows Jessi's heart."

Both of us moms had tears in our eyes. The groom's mother,

Kim, leaned over to me and said, "Drew has been a good student of Jessi's heart." Drew's patient persistence made him a valedictorian of Jessi's heart, and Drew's preparedness to love our daughter made his perfect answers absolutely understandable. I know people who have been married more than three decades who wouldn't be able to correctly answer twenty questions about their spouses!

Boaz was a student of Ruth's heart in that he quickly ascertained her needs, quickly promised to take care of them, and quickly did! He protected her from harm, he soothed her fears, and he completed the legal legwork to marry her—all in a very short time! A lesser man would have taken no notice of this foreigner, wouldn't have thought about her safety, would have refused the hassle of taking on Ruth and her mother-in-law, and would have left the women to fend for themselves. Boaz did the opposite, showing himself sensitive, aware, and capable of great love. He was prepared to provide for her—a quality of a MWWF.

The Lord blessed me with a Boaz of a guy. When we first started dating, he called me his "princess." I was so embarrassed that I asked him not to call me a princess around anyone else. He asked why. I replied that he might see me as a princess, but I was not one. In that moment, I revealed my distorted view of myself. At that point, I saw myself as damaged goods because of my background of sexual abuse. Of course, I knew intellectually that Jesus had forgiven me my past when I was born again, but my emotions were lagging behind my theology.

A Boaz of a guy speaks and acts in ways that heal a wounded woman, treating her like a princess even if she doesn't see herself as one. We saw earlier that Ruth viewed

> Loving, merciful, and confident are the top three characteristics an ideal godly man should embody.
>
> —Nichole, grad student

herself as just a "foreigner," undeserving of Boaz's generosity. But Boaz honored Ruth's sacrifices: he noted her "kindness" in not chasing younger men, and he reassured her that he would act on her behalf.

A Boaz is quick to help. A Bozo couldn't care less.

A MWWF Is a Fighter of Battles

A sixth quality is valor. Boaz was an overcomer. He was never one to shrink from a challenge or let others do the fighting for him. We see this in the fact that he was wealthy. He had fought business battles to become successful. Second, he was single. In a marriage-oriented culture that considered sons as riches, he could have married any young woman. But he chose to remain single until the right woman came along. He fought the battles of loneliness and cultural pressure.

Caleb, a man who lived in Moses' time, was considered a great man of faith, and he also illustrates this vital quality for a MWWF. In fact, he set this high standard for anyone who would pursue Caleb's own daughter. His standard for a Man Worth Waiting For was one who had enough faith to conquer the enemy. Caleb was not willing to give his daughter in marriage to a man who could not overcome the opposition placed before him.

I did not have a Caleb for a father, a man who set such a high standard for any man who wanted to write me into his future love story. But you and I have a heavenly Father who has set the standard so high through the biblical precedent of Boaz that we don't have to settle for men who can't, by faith, conquer the city of the enemy—whether it is the enemy of sexual temptation, greed, or entitlement.

The battles a man wins before marriage are a forecast of the victories he will achieve after marriage. Caleb apparently knew this. "Caleb said, 'I will give my daughter Acsah in marriage to the one who attacks and captures Kiriath-sepher.' Othniel, the son of Caleb's brother Kenaz, was the one who conquered it, so Acsah became Othniel's wife" (Josh. 15:16–17 NLT).

We discover that not only did Othniel conquer a city to win the privilege of marrying Acsah, but the very faith that enabled him to conquer a city became the platform for a future assignment:

> The Israelites did evil in the sight of the LORD; they forgot the LORD their God and served the Baals and Asherahs [false gods of other countries]. The anger of the LORD burned against Israel so that he sold them into the hands of Cushan-Rishathaim king of Aram Naharaim, to whom the Israelites were subject for eight years. But when they cried out to the LORD, He raised up for them a deliverer, Othniel son of Kenaz, Caleb's younger brother, who saved them. The Spirit of the LORD came upon him, so that he became Israel's judge and went to war. The LORD gave Cushan-Rishathaim king of Aram into the hands of Othniel, who overpowered him. So the land had peace for forty years, until Othniel son of Kenaz died. (Judges 3:7–11)

What a man conquers before he is even married becomes a frame for future victory. Don't settle for a man who is not fighting the good fight of faith. The skirmishes he faces as a single man are only preparing him for the major wars that are ahead. A Bozo runs from conflict and battle. A Boaz faces and conquers it.

Jesus died on the cross to conquer sin and death for the sake of His bride (those who are His followers). Don't settle for a guy who isn't willing to boldly conquer the enemy in order to win the privilege of sharing his journey on this earth with you.

Frogs and Princes

My brother-in-law Gary went through a terrible divorce and business setback at the same time my younger brother John did. These men responded in entirely different ways to the challenges of marital and business trouble. One man threw himself at God, fought his failures, and grew through the unlikely route to joy— suffering (more on this in chapter 7). The other one, my younger brother, raised a gun to his head in response and ended his life.

I was absolutely stunned by my brother's response to personal loss. I couldn't help but notice the vivid contrast to my brother-in-law's life. As Gary began to grow and learn from his loss—as he faced his own failures and fought discouragement—I clearly saw a MWWF in training.

In my life at that time was a single woman who was like family to me. She and I had been the best of friends for more than three decades. My husband had led her to a personal relationship with Jesus when she was only fourteen. I had watched my precious friend struggle with her prolonged singleness but always end up on the contented side of God's script for her.

One summer, I began to consider the possibility that my dear single friend might be a wonderful prospect for my amazing brother-in-law. During a birthday party for my mother-in-law, I was washing dishes in the kitchen with Gary's two girls. I said to one of his daughters, "Have you ever thought about your dad dating DeDe?"

My niece squealed with delight and said, "Kelly and I have both suggested it to my dad, but he always says the same thing: 'Frogs don't get to date princesses.'"

I immediately said to Kim, "Your dad is not a frog! His spiritual growth just proves he is a *prince* of a man." In other words, a Boaz of a guy!

After we finished the dishes, I went looking for the man who thought he was a frog. I told him what Kim had shared with me. He chuckled and we chatted only a few moments, but it was long enough to convince Gary that he should pray about asking DeDe out for a date.

How did things go? A year later, my husband performed the wedding for his brother and DeDe. I was the matron of honor, and I cried tears of joy through the whole ceremony. I was watching my dearest friend—who was single until she was forty—marry a MWWF.

A Boaz will face his trouble with God's help and overcome it. He will be worthy of a Woman Worth Waiting For. A Bozo will let life's setbacks overcome him.

Remember, precious daughter of God: He plans for you *only* Boazes. If you find yourself with a Bozo, remember who chose him for you. And move on!

DISCUSSION QUESTIONS

- ❧ Whom would you most likely choose for a date—a prince or a farmer? Be honest!

- ❧ Love needs to be examined under the microscope of this question: *Is this person qualified to help me obey God?* Another way to phrase it: *Does this guy draw me closer to God or distract me from God?* Can you apply these questions to the guy you like? How does he measure up?

- ❧ Which Boaz qualities are most significant to you?

- ❧ Which Boaz qualities had you not considered before as important? Which quality doesn't seem significant to you at this time?

- ❧ Were you surprised that Boaz was raised by a former prostitute? *Judges 2; Matthew 1:5* Discuss the impact of one's background on meaningful relationships.

- ❧ Discuss the change that Jesus can make in a life, even the life of a harlot. *John 4; 2 Corinthians 5:17; Isaiah 54:4*

✿ 5

sexual and holy

The title of this chapter may seem like an oxymoron, but, in fact, it is the reality of the daily life of a Man Worth Waiting For. He understands that he is a sexual being, yet he keeps his sexual urges under control, because he is keenly aware that he is to be holy like the One who loves him for all eternity. The apostle Peter wrote, "Prepare your minds for action; be self-controlled. . . . Just as he who called you is holy, so be holy in all you do; for it is written: 'Be holy, because I am holy'" (1 Pet. 1:13, 15–16). This is another nonnegotiable quality for a MWWF.

In the sixties, when chants of love and peace sounded incessantly, there surfaced a reply to the irony of "free love." I heard this phrase as a sixteen-year-old new Christian: *Lust can't wait to get, but love can wait to give.* History has proven that love and peace are not without cost.

> What characteristics are you still striving to achieve in your personal walk with God? Habitually pure life, righteousness, trusting in God (choosing God's ways over the world's), and eternal vision . . . not immediate gratification.
>
> —Chad, architect

How can a person in love wait to give? Is it possible for a healthy male to contain his physical expression of love? How can love wait? Love's capacity to wait is energized by good character, which supports his wise choices. A man can be sexual and holy because he has been practicing self-control.

How do we know Boaz was morally pure? We know that he was a man of principle who followed God's laws. We know the Bible describes him as having noble character. We also know that he honored and protected women, as we've seen with Ruth. Therefore, Boaz was a moral man. Modern Boazes are too.

Time to Grow Up

Singleness is not a time for men to start or prolong adolescent habits of fooling around sexually with any available woman. I know that statement smacks up against the media that sells everything to everyone via the most successful marketing tool of sex. But a Boaz understands that a man needs to develop the capacity to postpone a present pleasure for a future fulfillment.

When I was in high school, most of the girls I knew had a crush on a guy named Ted. He started to date a San Diego college cheerleader named Claudia. They became the ideal couple we all looked up to.

One evening we were invited over to Claudia's house for pizza. When we arrived, we were thrilled that Ted was there. After eating pizza and dessert, suddenly Ted was saying good-bye to everyone. He spent a few extra minutes saying good-bye to Claudia. After he was gone we asked her, "Why did Ted leave so early?" She shared with us that Ted had said to her as he left, "I love you too much to stay late tonight. The temptation would be too great."

All of us just sighed, and I remember praying that night, "Lord, I want a man who so loves me that he will walk away rather than give in to the pressure of sexual temptation."

The authors of the book *Too Close, Too Soon: Avoiding the Heartache of Premature Intimacy,* Jim Talley and Bobbie Reed, teach that a couple dating seriously need to limit the time they spend together each week to keep their moral batteries charged up. To remain pure before marriage, a couple's moral batteries need to be fully charged at all times. Ted and Claudia knew and lived out this principle.

Vulnerability Alert

A Man Worth Waiting For knows that sexual vulnerability occurs in any serious dating relationship, especially when the couple has come through an emotional event or a challenging trial or disagreement. It is not surprising that many teens have sex after a big win or big loss of the football team. Consider all the teens who have sex at the prom—an exciting time, but also an emotional time as the high schoolers' years are coming to a close.

The Word describes a woman comforting a man whose mother had died. Isaac, the miracle son of Abraham and Sarah, was a favored only child. So when Isaac's mother, Sarah, died, Abraham sought a bride for his son. When Isaac's bride arrived, she was not only a God-sent complement but also a God-sent comfort (Gen. 24:67).

Though physical love can be comforting, before marriage, it can also be a disastrous choice.

Our son-in-law recognized sexual vulnerability. In the course of their engagement, Drew and Jessi encountered several challenges. During one particularly emotional discussion, Drew suddenly asked Jessi to go and get the comforter off her bed.

Jessi was surprised, but she went and got her bed duvet. When she gave it to Drew, he took it and wrapped it tightly around her. Then he said, "Now we can continue discussing this situation. I don't want to take a chance of our getting carried away sexually during such an emotionally charged conversation."

Months later, when Jessi shared this particular event, I just about had a cheering fit. Here was a young man in the twenty-first century who understood the sexual vulnerability that is inextricably linked to emotional situations. Drew wrapped Jessi in a green duvet lest he be tempted to violate their boundaries of moral purity before they were married. A modern Boaz raised in a sexually saturated society!

What Women Don't Comprehend

It doesn't matter how much education a woman has or doesn't have, this idea seems to elude most of them: a man who does not succeed in keeping his sexual urges under God's control

before marriage will not be successful controlling his im-
proper sexual urges after marriage. Thus "sexual and holy" is
an essential element of a MWWF. It is a dangerous principle
not to grasp. Premarital sex is a postdated check for marital
unfaithfulness!

What too many women misunderstand is that sexual temptation does not subside with marriage but actually increases
in a different context. Violating sexual boundaries before marriage is called *fornication*, and violating sexual boundaries after
marriage is called *adultery*. The key for marital faithfulness is
the premarital prep of self-control!

I was part of the teaching staff at a conference for professional athletes and their wives. A nationally known counselor
and sex expert also spoke. He started with a short quiz on
sexual honesty in one's marriage. Before he began reading
the questions, you could already feel the tension in the room.
Having worked with those couples for more than thirteen
years, I could read the surprise on several women's faces as
they and their husbands heard the questions. Here are some
of them:

☘ Do your eyes lock on every attractive woman you see?
☘ Do you find your wife less sexually satisfying than when
   you were first married?
☘ Do you seek out sexually arousing articles, magazines, or
   Web sites?

There were several more questions, and they caused so much
of a stir that we had to do hours of counseling with upset couples after the speaker finished. Wives were shocked that their

> What characteristics are you still striving to achieve in your personal walk with God? Living moment-by-moment under the Holy Spirit's control, asking God to help me live like who He says I am already as His adopted son.
>
> —George Toles, marketing expert and former NBA broadcaster

husbands would be involved in anything that would compromise their sexual integrity.

The fact is, women are too often naïve when it comes to the sexual battle their husbands face every day. This battle begins when they're young men, continues while they are single, and follows right into marriage. Quite frankly, as long as there are breath and sperm in the man, he will face sexual temptation.

Consider the lengthy passages in Proverbs that warn men about sexual sin (6:20–7:27). Why does Proverbs have so many references to a man resisting the temptation of adultery? Because sexual temptation does not subside after a long honeymoon! "A man who commits adultery lacks judgment; whoever does so destroys himself" (Prov. 6:32).

And notice that when the early church was laying out the guidelines for godliness for the Greek converts, the sins the apostles warned against were two key ones: idolatry and sexual sin: "It seemed good to the Holy Spirit and to us not to burden you with anything beyond the following requirements. You are to abstain from food sacrificed to idols . . . and from sexual immorality. You will do well to avoid these things" (Acts 15:28–29). How ironic that sex is now an idol in the U.S., even among some Christians.

Why is sexual self-control such a massive battle? One reason is that for many men sex becomes compensation for a lack of true self-worth. Because sex is a man's number-one need, it is easy for him to equate his need with his worth. Society has told men a lie that his ultimate value is tied up with not only financial success but also sexual prowess.

Too often a man will not allow God to show him his true self-worth. Instead of embracing God's view of him, he listens to his peers, coworkers, or even the media's definition of significance. A man will try to relieve poor self-esteem by overcompensating with financial and sexual achievement.

When sex is compensatory, it moves from its rightful place in a man's life to an idolatrous place that is most destructive. Jonah 2:8 warns, "Those who cling to worthless idols forfeit the grace that could be theirs." When sex becomes an addictive idol, a man walks in a graceless condition.

A MWWF will never sacrifice his moral purity for an idol. He centers his self-worth on what God says about him.

Self-Control 101

Sexual purity is not an archaic idea. Sexual purity is God's idea, and since God created sex, He knows the best attitudes and actions for His creation. So many singles challenge the concept of remaining pure until marriage. But a famous biblical single guy wrote an explicit instruction about God's will and sexual purity: "It is God's will that you should be sanctified: that you should avoid sexual immorality; that each of you should learn to control his own body in a way that is holy and honorable, not in passionate lust like the heathen, who do not know God; and that in this matter no one should wrong his brother or take advantage of him" (1 Thess. 4:3–6).

Notice the phrase "should learn to control his own body in a way that is holy and honorable." It is God's will that His followers learn to control their bodies. Bozos give in to their hungers, no matter what the cost. Men Worth Waiting For understand that sex has its place.

Actually, one of the fruits of the Holy Spirit in Christians is the fruit of self-control. God would not have commanded sexual self-control if it were impossible. It was commanded by the One who not only created sexual longing but who also gives the power to live it. Men Worth Waiting For know this and function by it.

Bouncing the Eyes in Rome

A Boaz even protects others' sexual purity! When the man who would become my husband, Ken, was a youth pastor, twenty-five of his teens joined some ninety adults on a trip to the Holy Land. At the end of their tour, the team went on to Rome, and as the group walked through the city, Ken seemed to be leading the teens in a zigzag formation. When I asked him why we were zigzagging through Rome, he said, "I am helping the guys dodge the invitations of prostitutes." I remember being so impressed and walking away saying to God, "Oh God, I want one like Brother Ken, and I am willing to wait."

The book *Every Man's Battle* describes a method of self-control called "bouncing the eyes": when a man sees a woman dressed provocatively or any seductive image, he should develop the holy habit of bouncing his eyes away from the woman or picture that just caught his attention. Men cannot keep from seeing visually stimulating women and pictures throughout the day, but they can train their eyes to bounce off whatever they see.

I saw my future husband use the "holy bounce" on our first date. When Ken opened the car door for me, instead of watching me get in, Ken held the door handle and looked away. I didn't ask him about this behavior until we had been dating for some time. When I did inquire about it, Ken explained, "Jackie, when a young lady is getting into a car, especially when she is wearing a dress, she has to straddle the seat to get in the car, and I do not want to look up her dress."

I was blown away. I had spent so much of my life with guys hoping to see a "little skin," and here I was dating a young man committed to sexual purity in the simplest of situations. Ken had made a covenant with God not to lust after other women. This was a source of great self-control and has helped maintain our security for over thirty-one years of marriage.

Such behavior may seem like something out of the Puritan era, but not long ago I saw it demonstrated by a senior in high school. This young man, David, was playing the Beast in *Beauty and the Beast*. During one of the dress rehearsals I was watching, there was a scene where the Beast is supposed to lean into Beauty as she reads about King Arthur. No sooner had David stepped up on the little ottoman where Beauty was reading than he jumped off, as if he had just stepped on a tack.

Later, I heard the director ask him why he jumped off the ottoman so suddenly, and his reply wowed me—as my husband had wowed me twenty-eight years previously. David said, "I jumped back because Jessi's dress had not finished being fitted, and it was sticking out in the front a little. I didn't want to

> have really seen a red flag on occasions when all a guy focuses on are my physical characteristics.
> —Kathy Edwards, nurse

take the chance of looking down her dress."

Talk about the response of a Man Worth Waiting For. Yes, they do exist, and they are worth waiting for!

In several different sports, athletes must wear protective eye gear. Job 31:1, when memorized and lived out, combined with the holy habit of "bouncing the eyes" becomes a kind of protective eye gear. Just as a man will wear protective equipment for his sport, every man should add the Job 31:1 brand of eye gear to his "uniform" to keep him focused consistently on the goal and off the ever-present, superficial distractions of a sex-saturated society: "I made a covenant with my eyes not to look lustfully at a girl."

One day our son was watching TV as he was putting on his tennis shoes, getting ready to go to the gym to work out. As I was walking through the living room, I noticed a very provocatively dressed girl in a typical commercial on the sports station. It grieved my heart that a young man cannot escape such images on TV. Then I noticed something: our son was keeping his head down and apparently focused on his socks. He would lift his head to look at the TV momentarily, then bounce his eyes back to his socks and tennis shoes. I noticed that he did not lift his eyes until the commercial ended. Like his father, he had learned the "bounce the eyes" method, and he had put on the Job 31:1 protective eye gear even while watching *SportsCenter*.

Consider the guy you like. How does he act around provocatively dressed women? How does he act around you? Does he look women in the eyes when he speaks to them, or does he focus on their physical assets?

More Dangerous than the Nuclear Bomb

Regularly in the news, someone refers to weapons of mass destruction. Whether in the Middle East, Europe, or Asia, a concern exists about the possibility of an enemy having and using such weapons against us.

> What characteristics are you still striving to achieve in your personal walk with God? Deeper intimacy spiritually with God and constantly guarding my heart.
> —Terry Turner, senior vice president in sales and marketing

I see a weapon of mass destruction that has been unleashed through technology and I think it is more lethal than the nuclear bomb: the technological advances that now allow people to download porn to phones and iPods. People today are being effectively seduced by thousands of images and offers on porn Web sites. This seduction is not happening in dark, secluded back alleys, but in homes, in business offices, and even in parsonages.

The speed of porn distribution throughout the universe and the consequences of such a steady diet of soul-killing entertainment require a serious task force to combat porn. The apostle Peter spoke about such temptations: "Dear friends, I urge you, as aliens and strangers in the world, to abstain from sinful desires, which war against your soul" (1 Pet. 2:11). This powerful warning is absolutely relevant to us in the twenty-first century. To many singles—only Bozos, of course—the word "abstain" is repulsive. They see it as an impossible ideal left over from an ancient time. The word "abstain" here actually presents the idea of "distancing oneself" from the temptation.

How does one successfully war against those things that attack his soul daily? Matthew Henry said, "The joy of the Lord will arm us against the assaults of our spiritual enemies and put our mouths out of taste for those pleasures with which the tempter baits his hooks." In our sex-saturated society, we can see how people are so easily baited by the elaborate lure of lust. I believe men are easily assaulted by sexual temptation because they have never discovered the true joy of the Lord and they are not walking in that soul-strengthening joy. A college student paraphrased author John Piper's definition of sin this way to me: "Sin is what a person does when he is not satisfied with God."

One man told me, "I have had my struggles with pornography off and on throughout my life. Thank the Lord I have been clean now for almost five years. But every Saturday night, I get down on my knees and thank God that He got me through another week without using pornography. This is because I know this is a weakness of mine and that I must always be diligent and asking God for help in this area."

Take another look at the guy you like. Is he full of the joy of the Lord—or of a desire to get his hands on you?

To resist temptation, men need to fill their souls with enough of God's Word that they aren't lured into such deceptive arenas of pleasure. People are the sum total of all they read and understand. In Nehemiah we read:

Ezra [the scribe] opened the book [of the Law] . . . and as he opened it, the people all stood up. Ezra praised the LORD, the great God. . . .

They read from the Book of the Law of God, making it clear and giving the meaning so that the people could understand what was being read. . . . Nehemiah said, . . . "This day is sacred to our LORD. Do not grieve, for the joy of the LORD is your strength." . . . Then all the people went away to eat and drink, to send portions of food and to celebrate with great joy, because they now understood the words that had been made known to them. (Nehemiah 8:5–6, 8, 10, 12)

What are the top three characteristics an ideal man should embody? The three H's: honesty, hunger for the Word of God, and humility.
—*Victoria Rose, limited partner/owner of the New York Yankees*

Saturating yourself in God's Word results in exploding fireworks of joy that will keep you immune to one of Satan's brightest lures—sex.

Battle for the Thought Life: Boaz and Bozo

I remember the burst of giggles that filled a room of teenagers at summer camp when my husband and I were teaching on sex and we asked the kids, "What is the most powerful sex organ?" Of course, they didn't think of our answer—*the mind.*

There truly is a daily battle for our minds. For a guy to be sexual and holy in our sex-saturated society, his efforts will be equal to nothing less than fighting in a war. Daily we see pictures in the news concerning the various wars all over the world. Every time you see an image of a battle scene, you need to realize that such a battlefield is, spiritually speaking, in the mind of every guy you know.

A Man Worth Waiting For understands that this battle for his mind is as serious as the conflict in the Middle East. A MWWF is a wise man who has grasped the power of a mind dominated by love for God. The adolescent Bozo, on the other hand, strolls into the trap of lust, creating consequences graver than he could ever anticipate.

Look what Solomon wrote:

> At the window of my house
>   I looked out through the lattice.
> I saw among the simple,
>   I noticed among the young men,
>   a youth who lacked judgment. . . .
> Then out came a woman to meet him. . . .
> With persuasive words she led him astray;
>   she seduced him with her smooth talk.
> All at once he followed her
>   like an ox going to the slaughter . . .
>   little knowing it will cost him his life.
>   (Proverbs 7:6–7, 10, 21–23)

We have to understand, a Bozo is simply an adolescent who never learned to control his desires. He has lost the battle for his mind; he surrendered to the enemy without even putting up a fight. He grew up assuming that he had no power to control what his mind focused on, that he is an innocent victim of his urges and can't be held responsible for the kaleidoscope of lust-filled pictures that dominate his mind daily. Shakespeare understood this battle for the mind when he wrote: "My thoughts were like unbridled children, grown too headstrong for their mother."

Paul, a single guy and the greatest apostle, wrote about this battle for the mind. He knew about the

> The top three characteristics for a godly man are commitment (to the Word of God), purity (whether married or single), and humility.
> —Jessi, newlywed and seminary student

restless child who would demand control rather than be controlled by God's Holy Spirit: "We demolish arguments and every pretension that sets itself up against the knowledge of God, and we take captive every thought to make it obedient to Christ" (2 Cor. 10:5).

This battle for the minds of men is the key to their victory over the myriad of sexual temptations they face daily. When a man does not demolish the pretentious lusts that would seduce him, he may someday sell out his life for mere minutes of pleasure.

Men Worth Waiting For exhibit self-control in all they do: what they read, what they watch, what kind of friends they have, how they treat women. Bozos are all hands, all eyes, and all seductive talk. As I've said before, they're not interested in your company; they're interested in your body.

Bozos and Booze

I could write a separate book of horror stories I've heard about reckless actions between men and women because of alcohol. I will not spend too much time on this premise; suffice it to say, a woman (young or old) who is intoxicated is a perfect match for a Bozo. Be assured: Bozos are watching for women who like to overdo it.

Booze makes Bozo men courageous enough to disregard a woman's "no," even if she says it a dozen times. Booze has too often been the stimulus for Bozos to consider the unthinkable: to rape a drunken girl or to drug a girl to get sex. What would produce such boldness and perversion? An age of no standards—we are so enlightened, yet simultaneously so blind.

At present, I have three precious single girls in my life who were all raped during a drinking party. I know that thousands of girls can go to a party and not be raped, but my friends never even considered the lethal combination of Bozos and booze.

One young man I know wisely says, "When a girl goes to a frat party or even a bar, for her safety she needs to walk in with a bottle of water and consume only that. She should carry her bottle of water around like a security blanket." Girls have more to lose than a credit card when they are around the lethal combination of Bozo and booze. Better yet, women should opt for better places to meet men than bars and frat parties! Where do you think you'll find potential Men Worth Waiting For? Go there instead!

Wisdom Exchanged for Women

The wisest man who ever lived wrote:

> *I find more bitter than death*
> *the woman who is a snare*
> *whose heart is a trap*

and whose hands are chains.
The man who pleases God will escape her,
but the sinner she will ensnare.

(Ecclesiastes 7:26)

Now consider the reason for his statement. Scripture tells us:

> King Solomon . . . loved [felt a vehement inclination to] many foreign [wayward, alien] women besides Pharaoh's daughter—Moabites, Ammonites, Edomites, Sidonians and Hittites. They were from nations about which the LORD had told the Israelites, "You must not intermarry with them, because they will surely turn your hearts after their gods." Nevertheless, Solomon held fast to them in love. He had seven hundred wives of royal birth and three hundred concubines [lovers], and his wives led him astray. As Solomon grew old, his wives turned his heart after other gods, and his heart was not fully devoted to the LORD his God. (1 Kings 11:1–4)

How could such a smart man allow wayward women to turn his heart away from the true God who had blessed him so extravagantly with wealth, fame, and the greatest wisdom on earth? What has the power to seduce a man's heart away from his commitment to his Maker and Provider? It is so simple: vehement commitment to women and their sexual charms. No wonder Solomon wrote sarcastically: "While I was still searching but not finding—I found one upright man among a thousand, but not one upright woman among them all" (Eccl. 7:28).

Thousands of years later, we can learn from Solomon's poor example. In this chapter I've tried to give you the tools to sort Boazes from Bozos in the nonnegotiable quality of sexual self-control. If you can use these tools habitually, you will be the upright woman Solomon searched for—and a Boaz will find you.

DISCUSSION QUESTIONS

- ✿ Is it possible to be sexual and holy? *1 Corinthians 6:18–20* If so, how? What are some moral boundaries you have set up in your life?
- ✿ Premarital sex signs a postdated check for marital unfaithfulness. Agree or disagree? *1 Thessalonians 4:3–8*
- ✿ Discuss the long-term effects one moment of lust can create.
- ✿ Do you know guys who "bounce their eyes"?
- ✿ Do you know a victim of Bozo and booze—do you have a friend who was taken advantage of while she was intoxicated? What was the result?
- ✿ Is there a guy you like right now? What signs does he give of being sexual and holy?

✿ 6

emotional maturity

A man who loves others well is a man who understands the biblical premise of esteeming another person more important than himself (see Phil. 2:3). A man who assumes that the whole world revolves around him is a man who will love poorly and will probably be the poster child for the local tribe of Bozo guys!

I know that living in a self-enthralled, navel-gazing haze is not limited to the male gender. It just seems that the twenty-first century has increased the number of men who think such behavior is normal. The Me Generation has not left much room for a Man Worth Waiting For to even rent space here on earth. Our planet seems to be overpopulated with Bozo guys running in packs and encouraging the next generation to follow in their narcissistic footsteps.

As we begin to look at the emotional lives of a Boaz and a Bozo, I want to mention three deal breakers in male-female relationships. These qualities, if disregarded, will set a man and woman on an inevitable collision course with reality—and they may never recover from it. Women can sidestep a lifetime of unhappiness by merely being aware of these deal breakers and evaluating their boyfriends honestly. Incidentally, I got these ideas from a modern Boaz!

1. A MWWF has a growing relationship with Jesus and isn't just good at the Christian verbal dance.
2. A MWWF doesn't abuse substances or people.
3. A MWWF has personality quirks, but they're ones you can live with for a lifetime.

Because so many women disregard these three basic requirements, counseling practices are full and ministries have developed to work specifically with women who are suffering in fatally flawed relationships. A good friend of mine started a ministry called WAR (Women at Rest), which is for women who are spiritually mismatched. She teaches them how to face the daily battles that a spiritually unbalanced couple faces. When a woman ignores the deal breakers, she can count on frequent conflict, if not war, with her partner.

An Emotional Yardstick

We are going to look at different characteristics of emotional health, comparing the emotional instability of the Bozo and the growing emotional maturity of the Man Worth Waiting For.

We'll consider the negative Bozo quality first, followed by the contrasting positive quality of a Boaz.

A Bozo Is Controlled by His Emotions

Whether lustful, angry, moody, or demanding, a Bozo is an emotional cripple. Emotions dominate his life rather than his controlling his emotions with a principled character. Men rarely want to admit they're controlled by feelings, because they don't see themselves as emotional to begin with—they often think they're pretty disconnected from that aspect of their lives.

A guy suddenly gets angry and you think, *What just happened here? Did anybody see the change coming? Did I miss the warning that he was getting really angry?* Guys typically don't analyze situations that way. Something makes them angry and they react.

Professional counselors across America spend hours trying to help people connect with their emotions. You need to observe how the guy you like acts when things go wrong. If an event provokes disproportionate emotions, take note. Stress, frustration, and disappointment happen to everyone and may cause anger or moodiness, but everyone doesn't overreact.

I want to acknowledge that men do tend to be more objective. But a true problem is apparent when a man cannot even tolerate the presence of emotional expression. A man who is very nervous when someone is expressing pain, especially if tears begin to flow, will bristle and want to leave the scene immediately.

Consider the moodiness of Prince Amnon when he couldn't figure how to get what he wanted from Princess Tamar. And when she protested his disgracing the both of them, he still satisfied his ferocious lust. Then his feelings changed from "love" to hate. This was a man totally out of control.

Again, does the guy you like react sensibly and in proportion when bad things happen? If not—Bozo Alert.

A Boaz Is Patient and Self-Controlled

A Boaz is able to control his emotions; his emotions don't control him. He isn't detached from his emotions—some women mistake detachment for self-control. Unfortunately, many men who appear calm are really disconnected. When such men are married, their wives live with the daily frustration that they cannot experience any emotional intimacy with their husbands.

You see patient self-control when a man gets upset and knows what to do with the emotion. Some men use the women they're with as verbal punching bags for their strong feelings— these would be Bozos. Boazes feel the emotion, whatever it is—but they master it as well. They don't fly off the handle. They don't blame the women in their lives for their "bad luck." They don't take out what they feel on others. They know how to pause, breathe, and properly evaluate their responses.

Proverbs says, "Better a patient man than a warrior, a man who controls his temper than one who takes a city" (16:32). A Man Worth Waiting For is aware of the connection between an angry heart and offensive speech. He knows that the Holy Spirit wants to control his lips as well as his heart. Have you ever seen a simple discussion turn into a heated argument and you ask yourself, *What was that about?* Have you ever said something hateful, then immediately thought, *Where did that come from?*

Jesus told us what fuels harsh remarks and arguments: "For

out of the overflow of the heart the mouth speaks" (Matt. 12:34). If the guy you're dating or hope to date likes to start fights, hurts others when he's hurt, or shouts his anger at everyone—take note. He's probably a Bozo.

I know firsthand: anger and harsh remarks rise from an ailing heart. I struggled for many years with saying mean things and reacting angrily to people and situations. Then in Job I read, "What ails you that you keep on arguing?" (16:3). Talk about a searchlight being turned on in my soul! Suddenly I understood the source of the angry overflow: past hurt feelings from abuse, injustice, criticism, and rejection—all of these had been pressing on my heart, and the overflow was pungent. Forgiving so many who hurt me has helped my ailing heart get better, and my angry mouth and argumentative attitude are becoming more of a distant memory than a daily occurrence.

The next time you are with an angry or argumentative man, pray for insight into the things that have been pressing on his heart and causing such an overflow. If you know what's causing these behaviors, you may need to confront the man and encourage him to get help. If he doesn't—he's a Bozo. If he recognizes that he needs help *and* gets it, he's a Boaz. The past is not an excuse for our present anger, and it never justifies abusing people in the here and now. "My dear brothers and sisters, be quick to listen, slow to speak, and slow to get angry" (James 1:19 NLT).

A Bozo Believes He Is Entitled

A Bozo is angered when he doesn't get his way. His anger flows from a sense of entitlement. He wakes up in the morning focused on his wants and needs, and he rages whenever someone won't give him his way—24/7. He cannot handle disappointment and consequently, no one can handle him! The people around him walk on eggshells to accommodate him and prevent furious outbursts.

Bozos do not realize the danger of a self-centered existence. They do not correlate it with the anger that is a constant companion of the self-centered man.

How often do you get angry when things don't go the way you planned? In Numbers 20, we read that Moses and Aaron faced an angry crowd (more than two million strong) who were upset because of a life-threatening situation: no water in the middle of the desert. Moses and Aaron took this enormous need to God, and God told them exactly what to do: "Speak to that rock before their eyes and it will pour out its water" (Num. 20:8).

As Moses and Aaron gathered the grumbling people in front of the rock, a weary Moses struck the rock in anger (Num. 20:11). Moses' frustration with the whining chorus robbed him of the trust that he had demonstrated in the presence of Pharaoh as well as at the edge of the Red Sea. God said, "Because you did not trust in me enough to honor me as holy in the sight of the Israelites, you will not bring this community into the land I give them" (Num. 20:12). That passage breaks my heart, because I know that Moses took his eyes off the glory of God *just for a second* and focused on the whining community that was badgering him. The people's problem with trusting the God of Israel became Moses' problem. Moses let a mob of complainers yank his anger chain.

As I continued to examine Moses' struggle with anger, I saw that it was a symptom of his lack of trust. Now, whenever I am angry, I consider not only the person or circumstance but also the extent to which I am not trusting God.

Note: This was a Bozo moment in the life of a "friend of God" (James 2:23 NLT). Even a Boaz can have a Bozo moment.

Bozos focus on what they want and explode when they don't get it. But a better man behaves with more maturity. Read on!

A Boaz Can Rise Above Disappointment and Frustration

What lifts a Boaz above disappointment when he faces it? He has two qualities that are produced internally by God's Spirit—faith and peace. That means he has faith in a God who's bigger than whatever he confronts. When he faces disappointment, instead of responding angrily, he will pray, "Father, by faith right now I choose to believe You can bring good out of this." That expression of faith allows Jehovah-Shalom to give peace in the place where anger could have easily taken residency. Isaiah wrote, "You will keep in perfect peace him whose mind is steadfast, because he trusts in you" (Isa. 26:3).

A Bozo Doesn't Notice Others' Needs

I touched on this in an earlier chapter, but I want to reiterate it here as a measure of a man's emotional maturity. A Bozo can be in a room with a distraught person, and he doesn't even know that person's there. When someone mentions concern for a struggling person, he is absolutely stunned that a need even exists: "Is someone upset?" Such a man is absolutely comfortable with ignoring the needs of others. This behavior contradicts many Scriptures, such as: "If you see your brother's donkey or his ox fallen on the road, do not ignore it. Help him get it to its feet" (Deut. 22:4). Being sensitive to the needs of others is

The ideal man is honest, comfortable with himself, others-focused, and a servant leader.

—David Faison, CLU, chartered financial consultant, Northwestern Mutual

a compassionate response to what Paul called the "law of Christ": "Carry each other's burdens, and in this way you will fulfill the law of Christ" (Gal. 6:2).

A Boaz Focuses on Others

Remember Boaz's first response to the foreigner Ruth? He chose to protect and provide for her. A Boaz is capable of not only noticing the needs of others but also moving into action in response. He's courteous and always aware of those around him. This doesn't mean he tries to take care of everybody's needs, but he does what he can. This others-centeredness manifests itself in a fruit of Spirit: kindness. A Boaz has a way of going the extra mile.

For example, when my brother-in-law started dating my best friend, she was so impressed with how kind and courteous he was not only to her, but also to her mom who had been recently widowed. My best friend had been single for forty years, so she knew that guys could turn on the chivalry when they were trying to impress their dates and drop it just as easily. Gary maintained a steady courtesy that spoke volumes to my friend.

Remember, guys can turn it on for you—some (the Bozos) play at love so they can get the payoff. They can focus on you. Don't be impressed with that. Watch how he treats the person on the other side of you—your mom, sister, or even your best friend. Paul wrote, "Each of you should look not only to your own interests, but also to the interests of others" (Phil. 2:4).

A Boaz actually thrives on serving others. The joy of the Lord is his strength!

During one spring break, we were having a dinner party for seven college girls who were in West Palm Beach for vacation. I had met these girls at Liberty University when I spoke in chapel. When I told Ken about their coming for dinner, he said he was going to dress up in a tuxedo and serve dinner. I giggled and asked, "Why do you want to do that?" He replied, "Jackie, I want these young women to see that a good and healthy marriage is about mutually serving one another. I fear that these girls may have the impression that serving and hospitality are exclusively for a woman."

When the girls arrived, Ken greeted them at the door in his tux, and the girls were giddy within moments of entering our home. As Ken waited on all the girls throughout the meal and cleaned the dishes afterwards, the girls were all stunned. At the end of the evening I told the girls that a good man—a Boaz—is willing to serve alongside his wife. Then I challenged the girls to expect such humble servanthood from the men they dated. Only a Bozo would think serving is too feminine for a real man. Matthew wrote of Jesus, "The Son of Man did not come to be served, but to serve, and to give his life as a ransom for many" (20:28).

Remember the blessing that Boaz's workman called out to him when he arrived to examine the harvest? The workman asked God to stoop down and bless Boaz. That is the result

> The top three characteristics that an ideal godly man should embody: humility, servant's heart, and loving.
>
> —Garrett McAnear, dentist

of an others-centered employer. Boaz was meek. Being meek means that you're strong enough to be teachable and adaptable. This soul strength actually energizes a person's capacity to do for others with freedom.

My friend, bestselling author Chuck Snyder, gave me this definition:

> An ideal man . . . is the family provider, servant, and protector. God watches us when we watch over our wives and children. We pray for them and we put them first in everything: our time, our resources, and our patience. We make them laugh. We hold them when they cry. We control our anger. We are generous with our money. We are unselfish. We run from temptations of all kinds. We are loyal. We teach that love is a decision, not a feeling. We keep a promise. We are not critical. We do not hold grudges. We are merciful. We can have joy through the tears. We try not to be irritable or touchy. We are teachable.

As I think about Ken's servant's attitude, I think of Jesus and His coming to earth. Talk about humbling servanthood: from a smelly stable to a dusty carpenter's shop to meals with people whose souls needed major cleaning! In fact, in comparison to heaven, earth might have been like a big toilet. But "Jesus, the author and perfecter of our faith, . . . for the joy set before him endured the cross, scorning its shame, and sat down at the right hand of God. Consider him who endured such opposition from sinful men, so that you will not grow weary and lose heart" (Heb. 12:2–3).

A Bozo requires everyone around him to serve him. A Boaz is eager to serve others. Ken has always had such a servant's heart. The Bible commands a wife to respect her husband (Eph. 5:33), and Ken's behavior makes it easy for me to do that. You will admire a Boaz's attitude and actions toward others. If a man lives to be served, let the Bozo find some other girlfriend to do it for him.

A Bozo Is Quick to Criticize Others

A Bozo is very critical. He is not a happy camper and neither are those who have to digest a steady diet of his critical appetizers. Some of us had fathers who were very critical, and if we don't let Jesus heal those wounds in our hearts, we may embrace the attention of a Bozo with a critical spirit.

With this guy, failure is fatal. He is not emotionally secure enough to handle disappointments in his own life. The fact is, only when I can handle failure in my own life am I compassionate about the flaws in others. The person with a critical spirit hasn't learned that, because of God's grace, failure is never fatal.

A Boaz Is Tolerant of Flaws

When you are understanding of your own flaws and know that God forgives you for them, you don't need to put others down to feel good about yourself. Criticizing others is simply a way of affirming oneself. The more insecure a man is, the more addicted he is to judging people. A Bozo would never consider the hurts and needs of others—he would criticize them for their flaws! But look at Boaz. Rather than criticize Ruth's background as a Moabitess, a woman from the idol-worshiping

An ideal man is loving, dependable, and passionate.

— Tim, self-employed, postal worker, basketball referee

and enemy country Moab, he had compassion for her and immediately provided for her needs.

I heard Christian comedian Ken Davies say on the radio, "I'm not okay, you're not okay, but that is okay!" Now there is a guy who understands that imperfection is part of life on earth. Our son told me about something Bono, from the band U2, said. It was something like this: "The Bible is brimful of hustlers, murderers, cowards, adulterers, and mercenaries and that used to shock me. Now it is a source of great comfort." The reality that God used imperfect people throughout the ages should be a comfort to all of us. Consider the example of tolerance displayed brilliantly in Jesus. Tolerance permeated Jesus' life and kept Him from incinerating the people who spoke so arrogantly against Him!

A Bozo Has a High Opinion of Himself

Some men actually believe God gave them all insight. They think they're Solomon's descendants and that their great wisdom draws the only right conclusion in a matter. When you hear someone speak up this confidently, at first you may think, *Wow, does that guy have conviction and commitment!* But if you listen long enough, his rigidity becomes more apparent. He's so rigid that if you bang into him he'll probably break into a thousand pieces.

I knew a pastor who was incredibly opinionated, and many people in our town were impressed with his "high ideals." As people I knew began to flock to his church, I told my friends,

"You need to buy a spare set of seat belts." Why? I told each one of them that a man who is that rigid and perfectionistic is hiding a dark secret that will eventually be revealed.

Well, months later, in our local newspaper as well as on the evening news, the opinionated pastor was one of the top stories. This pastor got caught in a prostitution ring where he actually had driven the church van to pick up the prostitute. Hello! I got many calls from distressed church members who thought I was some kind of prophet. No, it is simple: the more perfect the picture presented, the darker the secret covered.

Have you met many people who are closed-minded and narrow? Some actually admire such rigidity and see it as strength. Too often people applaud this narrowness and ignore the harm that such self-confidence can cause. I know many people who have been broken by such rigidity.

Rigidity is a sure way to catch what I call the Galatian Virus, whereas a merciful heart is a sure immunization against it. I was introduced to this virus while attending one of the most legalistic Christian colleges in the United States. I spent four years observing how miserable Christians are when they live with too little grace and too much emphasis on the letter of the law. Paul warned, "You who would be justified by the law; you have fallen from grace" (Gal. 5:4 ESV). I spent four years trying to resist becoming infected with the Galatian Virus.

The Galatian Virus has noticeable symptoms: an infected person is drained of joy and creativity and is filled with cynicism. The virus erases a person's loving attitude and fills him instead with disdain for others. This disease-ridden individual often looks as if he sucks lemons on an hourly basis.

Throughout my four years of training, I learned how to

get immunized against this graceless condition. Whenever I noticed one of the symptoms coming on, I would reread the book of Galatians and the symptoms would subside. A Bozo embraces the Galatian Virus—he celebrates having it and tries to force others to get infected. A Boaz knows how to resist the Galatian Virus that would choke the grace of God from his heart.

A Boaz Has a Humble, Open Heart and Mind

When Boaz first inquired about the young woman working in his field, the men kept referring to her as "the Moabitess" who came to Bethlehem with Naomi. Boaz, being a principled man of the Word, knew what Deuteronomy said about Moabites: "You must never, as long as you live, try to help the Ammonites or the Moabites in any way" (Deut. 23:6 NLT). If Boaz had been an opinionated man, he never would have thought to take extra care of Ruth. He would have justified his insensitive behavior by quoting the Law.

But Boaz knew the whole story about Ruth's choosing to leave her people and the gods of Moab for the people of Israel and the one true God. Her conversion to the Hope of Zion caused Boaz to respond with openhearted mercy rather than with rigid rejection. Boaz surely lived out this verse from Micah: "He has showed you, O man, what is good. And what does the LORD require of you? To act justly and to love mercy and to walk humbly with your God" (Mic. 6:8).

Boaz's humble, open heart and mind made him approachable. His employees respected him, and Ruth was awed by him. Boaz revealed his heart when he responded to Ruth's request to be her kinsman-redeemer. He acknowledged that he wasn't the youngest or necessarily the most desirable guy in the neighborhood. And he wasn't afraid to admit it!

A Bozo thinks he knows everything and so considers himself very important. A Boaz recognizes his imperfections and humanity, and *others* consider him important.

A Bozo Has Excuses for Not Doing a Task

What's scary about a man who always has excuses for what he didn't do or finish is that he is always looking for a new team member—someone to accept and relay his excuses. If you marry such a man, you become part of the excuse team. You will be the wife on the phone making excuses to his boss, his mother, and even his friends. Then you will have children and *they* will join the Bozo excuse team, having grown up watching Mom do it. This effective team of enablers reinforces the Bozo's behavior, so he is never accountable for the way he lives. A Bozo is ineffective at many things and always has a "good reason" for it.

A Boaz Works to the Best of His Ability and to Jesus' Glory

Boaz was successful because he was not intimidated by having to strive and persevere—whether in famine or plenty. Naomi and her husband left Bethlehem during a difficult time of famine and went to Moab. How tragic that in an attempt to escape the hardship of famine, not only Naomi's husband died in Moab, but so did her two sons—just after having married. Boaz stayed behind in Bethlehem and worked the land even during a difficult time. He didn't sit back and make excuses for why he couldn't produce a crop. Boaz's persistence would bless not only his employees but also eventually Ruth and Naomi. Boaz understood the payoff of "long obedience in the same direction," as Eugene Peterson puts it. Boaz strove to work to the best of his ability, and that's the fruit of Spirit—faithfulness.

Some men work to the best of their ability to secure glory for themselves. They want more attention, more applause. It's so refreshing to be around a gifted man who is humble about what God has entrusted to him. Hard work coupled with humility starts young in the heart of a Boaz.

There are many Bozos out there because they have not had emotional maturity fleshed out by their fathers or other male leaders in their lives. Yes, I feel sorry for those guys. But don't date a guy because you feel sorry for him. "Mercy dating" can end in a very pathetic marriage. I have heard so many single girls say, "Oh, I feel so sorry for him, I'll go out with him again." Invite him to church, pray for him, but don't mercy-date him!

A Bozo Lacks Integrity

Whatever dictionary you use, you will find *integrity* commonly defined as "honesty" and "strong moral principles." Consider Prince Amnon, the leader of the Bozo tribe; you would never describe him as a man of integrity. Prince Amnon was strongly committed to satisfying himself—his adherence was to bow before his heart's lust rather than bow before God's moral code.

The term *integrity* has become somewhat clichéd in the last decade. It has been overused and often misapplied. Often I have heard people say, "Oh, he's a man of such integrity." Yet I would think, *He may have moral uprightness, but he's not real nice about it.* To me, if a guy has good character and moral integrity, he will be kind, merciful, and gentle.

We need to be careful about throwing that word around. Sometimes men of "great integrity" speak to their wives with contempt. How a man treats his wife—or his girlfriend—is a great calibrator for whether or not he is a Bozo.

A Boaz Is a Classic Example of Integrity

From the moment Boaz enters the short love story of Ruth, his responses to his employees and then to the foreigner Ruth are a brilliant display of adherence to God's principles. Boaz understood sacrificial love. His integrity made him capable of dying to himself and his desires. When Ruth came to the threshing floor to ask Boaz to be her kinsman-redeemer, Boaz responded with principled integrity: "Although it is true that I am near of kin, there is a kinsman-redeemer nearer than I. Stay here for the night, and in the morning if he wants to redeem, good; let him redeem. But if he is not willing, as surely as the LORD lives I will do it" (Ruth 3:12–13). When Ruth told Naomi what he said, Naomi replied, "Now be still, the man will not rest until he has taken care of us." She knew integrity when she saw it.

Boaz was willing to go to the city gate and talk to the kinsman who was the more rightful heir to this responsibility. Why was Boaz so willing to do all this for Ruth and Naomi? I've mentioned that Boaz was not only driven by his own integrity but he was also stimulated by Ruth's integrity. He talked about this irresistible force: "Now, don't worry about a thing, my daughter. I will do what is necessary, for everyone in town knows that you are an honorable woman" (Ruth 3:11 NLT).

To a Boaz, a woman with equally strong character makes her "simply irresistible." Are you that woman?

DISCUSSION QUESTIONS

- ✿ Discuss the relational deal breakers. Can you think of any additional relational deal breakers?
- ✿ When considering the premier signs of emotional maturity, which one is the most significant to you?
- ✿ Do you see emotional immaturity in any of the guys you know or date? What does this tell you about their character?
- ✿ Do you know an exception to this emotional immaturity—maybe someone at work, in your community group, at church? Describe him. Give an example of his maturity and explain how it impressed you.
- ✿ Did this chapter cause you to consider your own emotional maturity? Discuss how a person's heart wounds may impact what kinds of guys she pursues.
- ✿ Have you considered the correlation between emotional maturity and the fruits of the Holy Spirit? *Galatians 5:22–23* Talk about how you will work to develop this maturity in yourself—and hold out for a guy who shows it in his life.

&7

courage in suffering

I don't necessarily enjoy sports on TV, but I do like watching the last few minutes of an event. I have always enjoyed seeing a man's response when he wins or loses. On Sunday, July 23, 2006, I was washing dishes and catching the last few minutes of the British Open. When Tiger Woods won, he turned to give a celebration hug to his caddy. The hug lasted longer than one would have expected. Then the camera moved in closer and I could see that Tiger had started to weep. My husband explained that Tiger's dad had died, so Tiger wouldn't be receiving his usual congratulatory hug from his dad.

Tiger did not simply tear up, he wept, and his tears continued as his inner circle greeted him as he walked off the golf course. Of course I was tearing up also. I watched as each person wept and hugged Tiger. I was totally impressed with the emotional freedom Tiger's inner circle gave him. His trainer, coach, and wife all embraced him and his tears.

Later in an interview Tiger said, "I could not hold back the tears anymore, I miss my dad so much." One of the greatest athletes in the world couldn't avoid showing his pain, though he tried.

For me, Tiger Woods won more than the British Open that Sunday. Tiger grew in courage as a man to express his true feelings, even if they provoked tears. There were two "Opens" that Sunday: the British Open and the Heart Open!

Being a woman, I am cognizant of the terror that men feel in relation to the "icky" feelings that may flow if they ever allow themselves to look at their heart wounds. A Man Worth Waiting For has the nonnegotiable quality of courage to examine the wounds he carries in the deepest parts of his heart. He even invites God into the process: "Search me, O God, and know my heart; test me and know my thoughts. Point out anything in me that offends you, and lead me along the path of everlasting life" (Ps. 139:23–24 NLT).

One of my favorite young men, Cody McQueen, reflected:

> When David asked the Lord to search his heart and find any offensive way in him in Psalm 139, he was asking the Lord to know him in order that he may know God. As men in the twenty-first century, we have become very good at masking who we are. We have been told we are to be the strong ones, the providers, and the rocks of our families, businesses, and friendships. But so often we are trying to maintain our façade of stability while ignoring the shaky ground that is the "bedrock" of our souls.

A Boaz is willing to go to the inmost place for any heal-ing or renovation needed to be the best image-bearer on earth. "Surely you desire truth in the inner parts; you teach me wis-dom in the inmost place" (Ps. 51:6).

A MWWF Doesn't Fear Tears—His or Others'

I wonder if, when King David heard that his firstborn, Prince Amnon, had raped Princess Tamar, he practiced that manly habit of disconnecting his head from his heart. The Scripture says David was "furious" about it, but he did nothing. In fact, one translation says, "but David did not grieve the spirit of Amnon his son, for he loved him because he was his firstborn."[1] I think denial is the ability to disconnect the head from the heart.

When Tamar's brother Absalom found out what happened, he said something that reflects the head/heart disconnection and reveals the "fixer" tendency in all men. They'd much rather fix the problem than act as compassionate listeners and com-forters. He saw Tamar weeping and said: "Has that Amnon, your brother, been with you? Be quiet now, my sister; he is your brother. Don't take this thing to heart" (2 Sam. 13:20).

Don't take it to heart. Excuse me, but a woman can't keep rape from invading her heart! Sexual abuse is a soul-killing crime. I have watched men who are so uncomfortable with a weeping woman that they spurt these phrases. But like David, these men don't really help.

Ironically, Absalom told Tamar to be quiet while a volcano began to surge within his own heart. Disconnection between the head and heart often leads to a volcanic eruption. Emotions can't stay stuffed or ignored forever. Absalom arranged for the murder of his brother. Anger held in fermented into murder.

If David and Absalom had not reverted to the easy disconnect from their hearts, something wiser could have been done about Amnon's rape of Tamar.

Record of a Warrior's Tears

Look at these verses: "Record my lament; list my tears on your scroll—are they not in your record?" (Ps. 56:8) and "Morning, noon and night I plead aloud in my distress, and the LORD hears my voice" (Ps. 55:17). These verses were not written by a melancholy woman but by the great warrior poet of Israel, King David. David was a brave leader who so inspired his army that they would gladly die in battle for him. This warrior was not afraid of the battle in the wilderness or the battle within his soul. He was a man not paralyzed in the presence of tears or ashamed of his own. This makes his lack of reaction in the Tamar incident even more baffling.

I have seen a man paralyzed by tears. A man and his wife came over for dinner. While we were talking, the wife began to weep. Her husband sat stone-faced. Ken and I both jumped up to hug her and pat her on the shoulder.

I know people have different attitudes about the public expression of emotion. I have probably made thousands uncomfortable with my emotional freedom. But even Jesus wept, and I know that God would not have created humans with tear ducts if we didn't need an emotional release once in a while. He knows our heads and hearts must be connected if we're to be healthy people—and compassionate people.

A MWWF Doesn't Prolong His Adolescence

A Man Worth Waiting For resists using superficial anesthetics for comfort when suffering. He has learned to reach for God's Word rather than the TV remote. Why are so many men afraid to become theologians through suffering? I heard author Dan Allender say at a seminar, "Suffering is an unlikely route to joy." Oh for the courage to become a theologian through suffering. One psalmist wrote, "Before I was afflicted I went astray, but now I obey your word. . . . It was good for me to be afflicted so that I might learn your decrees" (Ps. 119:67, 71).

A man can prolong his adolescence if he doesn't let his trials and suffering escort him deeper into God's heart and Word. A mature look at suffering and its balancing contribution to our maturity was captured in this reflection:

> *It feels right to me that life*
> *Must have balance, that good*
> *Times and hard times are*
> *Meticulously measured out, for it is*
> *Only in the blend of both*
> *That we grow . . .*
> *That wholeness comes,*
> *That we know how to laugh*
> *With others*
> *And how to cry.*
> *Substance in the human heart*
> *Is built . . . nurtured . . . so much*
> *More by pain and failure*
> *And disappointment*

> *Than by happiness and joy, yet God, in*
> *Infinite wisdom, understands what*
> *Our limits are and never*
> *Tries us more than we can handle.*[2]

When an adolescent suffers, he immediately searches for comfort and relief from suffering. He never considers what he might learn through suffering and he surely is not mature enough to observe what God might want him to unlearn through suffering. The techniques that teens use to anesthetize their pain often are the same ones they use when they become adults. This is a Bozo mentality at work, immaturity leading the way: deaden the pain, distract from the reality, whether through booze, drugs, porn, 24/7 sports, or Xbox. Women use some of these anesthetics, though their favorites are mall therapy, chocolate, and lengthy gab fests.

The only way to begin exiting the adolescent response to suffering is to begin to ask God, "What do You want me to learn through this?" A MWWF does this.

If the guy you like spends extreme amounts of time even on things as seemingly harmless as video games, take note. He may be a Bozo.

Our Son Exits Adolescence Through Suffering

While in college, our son Ben had been praying for a Bible study with older men. He was in a Bible study with his peers, but he wanted the accountability of those older and wiser. Ben attended a Pro Athletes Outreach (PAO) conference where the Lord allowed him to strike up a conversation with the chaplain for the Atlanta Braves, Tim Cash. Out of that discourse came an invitation to a Bible study with Tim and some older guys.

The first time Ben attended this group, the leader asked him to share a short testimony about his journey with Jesus. One thing Ben said, which the leader told me about later, has stayed with me: "I'd rather suffer with God than suffer without God." And then he shared a quote that he learned from Pastor Larry Wright: "I'd rather suffer obediently than prosper disobediently because I know my obedient suffering is as temporary as my disobedient prosperity."

As I pondered Ben's remark, I thought about Romans 8:18: "I consider [mental conclusion] that our present sufferings [misfortune] are not worth comparing with the glory [object of God's highest regard] that will be revealed in us."

God showed Ben that when severe pain entered his life, instead of continuing on his journey of faith, he raged in anger toward God and pulled away. Many, if not most, of us do the same at one time or another. Consequently his faith was shaken. When pain outruns our faith, bitterness enters the soul. Ben was so relieved when he finally understood the source of all the cynicism that had flowed into his heart.

Don't misunderstand: faith does not take the pain out of suffering, but faith prevents the infection of despair. A faith-filled person has an unimaginable capacity to face unimaginable suffering.

So does a Man Worth Waiting For.

Recently during an interview with a seminary professor, my daughter, Jessi, expressed her response to the suffering that took hold of our family in the early nineties—in that time period, we lost five family members, two by suicide—and escorted her out of adolescence. Jessi said, "During the horrible trials my family went through, my brother Ben raged against God and began to withdraw spiritually. I kept watching my parents as they threw themselves upon God during the terrible trials. I decided, *If my parents can hang on . . . so can I*." Our children embodied the two common responses to suffering: rage against God or throwing oneself against God and clinging with all you have.

A Man Worth Waiting For knows how to deal with pain. He lets it pull him toward God, rather than away from Him.

Courage to Face the Infamous "Father Wound"

For years I have felt that God created women to help men reconnect their heads with their hearts. At a conference, I heard a wonderful coach speak about his father screaming at him for crying as a little boy, saying that real men don't cry! Talk about a lie.

Let me give you an example of a father wound. Some years ago, Ken and I were to speak at a singles' conference on Marco Island. We planned to take both our children with us. Before we left for the conference, a little dilemma arose. Our Ben needed to be at the train station on Sunday to join his classmates for their sixth-grade trip to Washington, D.C. The singles' conference didn't end until Monday afternoon. Ken told the conference leaders he would start the workshop with me, but he would have to leave early so he could drive Ben home and to the train station.

Now, you are wondering, what does this have to do with a *heart wound*? And where in this story could the revelation of a heart wound from a father ever arise? And—what does this have to do with a Man Worth Waiting For? Keep reading.

We traveled to Marco Island. The conference started. As the room filled up for our workshop, our kids were supposed to come to the back when Ken and Ben needed to leave. So, Ken and I started teaching, and fifteen minutes into the workshop, in walked Ben and Jessica. When Ken spotted Ben with his suitcase, Ken stopped right in the middle of his statement and stepped from behind the podium.

He said, "I am going to leave before this workshop is done. I want you to know why I am leaving. I am not a man who would neglect his commitments, but today I am a father who is choosing time with his son over his work. I had a father who *never* chose me over work. In fact, my father would have never left a conference to drive me anywhere. Today I choose our son."

Well, when Ken said, "Today I choose our son," he began to cry. I was absolutely stunned, because I married the calmest man, and I wasn't sure I had ever seen him cry. Ben ran down the aisle and hugged his dad. Then the room full of single guys and girls started to cry—then burst into applause.

That was the first time my husband ever acknowledged he had a father wound. He lived in the same house with his father, but he never saw him until he was a teen, because his father was a workaholic. Thousands of children in America have been abandoned physically by their fathers through divorce, but thousands of sons have been abandoned emotionally by fathers who were physically present but emotionally unavailable. This is a wound that needs to be healed.

Cody McQueen shared these thoughts with me about a MWWF's need for courage.

A man cannot aspire to anything if he does not start with courage. [A] fierce task lies before any man who decides to lay down his life in a world that calls him to fight for everything he can get his hands on. This might seem to be a contradiction, since most people associate courage with fighting. In some cases this is true, but a man is also called to a courage that involves not physical fighting, but ultimate dying.

It takes a lot of courage to die, and that is what we are called to do as Christians (Luke 9:23–24). If a man wants to truly follow Christ, he must die to himself. He must die to his instinct to secure his future and hoard his possessions. He must not trust in his own abilities or his own cleverness to get what he wants. He must put others before himself even if it takes his time, energy, or finances.

Does the guy you like show signs of courage? Is he confident about taking a stand? Can he, like Ken, discern the important decisions from the trivial ones? Does he put others before himself?

A Man Cognizant of Emotional Issues: Cooper's Courage

My husband and I were in Europe during Hurricane Katrina, but the newscasts there were totally focused on the tragedy. One face kept appearing in many of the news stories. This one guy seemed to be brimming with empathy. This compassionate and passionate reporter was Anderson Cooper, host of CNN's *Anderson Cooper 360*.

A good friend told me she had heard Anderson interviewed on the radio, commenting on family and his painful past encounters. His father died when he was ten, and his brother committed suicide when Cooper was twenty.

Anderson is a man who has been escorted through pain into a public arena of empathy and insightful reporting that has captivated thousands. The pain he has experienced has allowed him to move and work in painful situations like war and natural disasters. He has harnessed the painful moorings of his soul and has become a compassionate witness to the suffering of others.

Anderson illustrates a key part of a Man Worth Waiting For. All of us will face pain, but the best of us will let it make us more compassionate. A man who is uncomfortable with suffering and the verbal expressions that flow from suffering would benefit from considering the fact that God never reprimanded Job for his despair-filled rants (Job 6:8–9), but God did reprimand his insensitive, self-righteous, preachy male friends (Job 42:7–8). Or consider David's emotional pleas in the Psalms. Clearly God does not disdain emotion.

Is the man you like able to talk about his emotions, about things that have hurt him in the past? If you recognize unresolved pain or anger in him, he's not ready to be your Boaz. If he deals with his "inside stuff," you will see a healthy, happy man who isn't afraid of talking about or showing emotion. Be careful. Be discerning. You have your own emotional stuff to deal with—a Man Worth Waiting For doesn't expect you to handle his as well.

DISCUSSION QUESTIONS

❧ Have you experienced a man's being uncomfortable around your tears? If so, give an example. Do you think this is a common response?

❧ Tears are not a "girlie" thing but also a warrior's experience. *Psalm 56:8* Discuss the stereotype and the biblical image countering it.

❧ Suffering escorts one out of adolescence. Discuss this idea in context of these verses: *Psalm 119:67, 71*

❧ If you bury a hurt, you also bury the hope of healing. Do you think the Christian community as a whole encourages men to bury their hurt?

❧ We read about Jesus: "When he drew near and saw the city [Jerusalem], he wept over it" (Luke 19:41 ESV). Discuss what that means for men today. Discuss how this affects your view of a Man Worth Waiting For.

♣ 8

reckless abandon

When I was in high school, a fresh wind of God's power began to move across the U.S. on college campuses and in high schools. This refreshing outbreak of God's presence among young people was later called the Jesus movement. I became a follower of Jesus during this time. What was distinctive about the Jesus movement was the radical response that young people were displaying in their passionate commitment to be like Jesus in a modern world.

Throughout my adventure with Jesus, many people have considered me radical—a "Jesus freak." I have never been ashamed of my reckless abandon to Jesus. I have always considered it a reasonable response to the incomparable gift of an intimate relationship with the Commander of a million stars.

This morning I was reminded of the difference between the

An ideal man is one whose love for the Lord pervades every part of his life.
—Douglas W. Rose, Campus Outreach staff, Virginia Tech

Jesus freaks and the ho-hum religious. Luke 17 tells the story of Jesus' healing the ten lepers. Only one returned to acknowledge and thank Jesus for healing him: "One of them, when he saw that he was healed, came back to Jesus, shouting, 'Praise God, I'm healed!' He fell face down on the ground at Jesus' feet, thanking Him. . . . Jesus asked, 'Didn't I heal ten men? Where are the other nine?'" (Luke 17:15–17 NLT).

This former leper had a thank you that he couldn't contain, and he had to worship. The other nine lepers were healed physically but their souls remained in a leprous condition. How can I say that? In my almost four decades of walking with Jesus, the people I've met who live in reckless abandon to Jesus are "ex-lepers" who are obviously grateful that they have been healed. Reckless abandon to Jesus is not a result of mental imbalance but of a soul overflowing with such thankfulness to God that it results in this radical commitment to Jesus. Are you one of the healed lepers who didn't return in gushing gratitude, or are you a grateful Jesus freak because you realize the gift that you have been given?

Men Worth Waiting For Don't Just Feel—They Act

We've talked about the fact that men are often trained to be detached from their emotions. This means they may *feel* they should do something, but they ignore what they feel and, therefore, any nudge for action. I have watched hundreds of men listen to a plea for help for a very noble cause. The men look as if they are paying attention, and some may even appear empathetic. But when the meeting ends, most do not respond. They very calmly disregard the internal emotional nudge. Instead, they walk to their cars and head home to watch the highlights of the day, whether on the local news or the sports channel.

An ideal man is wise, loving, adventurous, assertive, controlled, sensitive, generous, humble, and a leader.
—*Whit, student at Dallas Theological Seminary*

A Bozo is moved to action but never follows through. A Boaz is moved and acts immediately, because he knows he can make a difference in someone's life by obeying his impulse.

Reckless Abandon and "Foolishness"

A twentieth-century martyr named Jim Elliot said, "He is no fool who gives what he cannot keep to gain what he cannot lose." Jim harnessed his emotions and responded courageously to God's call to reach the Auca Indians in Ecuador with the good news of Jesus. He and his teammates were martyred, but their deaths inspired many others to give their lives to God in missions and other noble purposes. In 2006, the story of these missionaries' martyrdom came to movie theaters in a film called *At the End of the Spear*.

Jim and his fellow missionaries were murdered in the early fifties, yet more than five decades later, their honorable life sacrifices continue to inspire people to obey God's nudges. Look at how Paul saw such dangerous assignments:

> And now, compelled by the Spirit, I am going to Jerusalem, not knowing what will happen to me there. I only know that in every city the Holy Spirit warns me that prison and hardships are facing me. However, I consider my life worth nothing to me, if only I may finish the race and complete the task the Lord Jesus has given me—the task of testifying to the gospel of God's grace. (Acts 20:22–24)

Men who choose to obey God despite their own fears or others' criticism are Boazes in the most heroic sense. Several of the newspapers and magazines referred to the missionaries' martyrdom as such "a waste of life." Many saw it as merely a foolish endeavor.

Paul the apostle is a classic example of a man who lived with reckless abandon and was considered foolish by many of those in his former circle of education, status, and influence. No wonder Paul impacted Christianity incomparably. His relentless pursuit of Jesus has been a beaming example through the centuries and has inspired young men and women to follow Jesus as he did.

Paul wrote, "If anyone else thinks he has reasons to put confidence in the flesh, I have more: circumcised on the eighth day, of the people of Israel, of the tribe of Benjamin, a Hebrew of Hebrews. . . . But whatever was to my profit I now consider loss for the sake of Christ" (Phil. 3:4–5, 7). Jim Elliot and Paul the apostle knew that in comparison to eternity, one's life is but a weekend. They were not going to waste their brief "weekends" here on earth. I believe their seemingly reckless passion probably received a standing ovation from the "great cloud of witnesses" in heaven (Heb. 12:1).

Matt Redman is the composer of the popular worship song "Blessed Be Your Name." He did not write this song in an ivory tower but in the crucible of a difficult life. His many trials as a young man growing up, coupled with more heartache in his marriage, are recorded in his book, *Blessed Be Your Name*. Matt learned while still young how to be fruitful in a time of suffering. His reckless abandon to Jesus is the foundation of his victory.

> The top three characteristics of an ideal man include the lifelong pursuit of God, a teachable spirit, and being willing to communicate.
> —O. S. Hawkins, president of Guidestone Financial Resources

Abandon to God's Script

A man of passionate faith is not just a stoic who pushes through life's challenges in his own strength. I have met so many athletes who, through discipline, have secured their places in history. The only problem with some of these achievers is the high price of a life that is all about them. With the man of passionate faith, the race is all about God. Oswald Chambers captured the noble life purpose of a man of reckless abandon—a Boaz—in one sentence from his devotional *My Utmost for His Highest*: "Joy comes from seeing the complete fulfillment of the specific purpose for which I was created and born again, not from suc-

An ideal man is first and foremost a follower of Christ who demonstrates dependability, trustworthiness, and consistency.

—*Eddie Taubensee, retired baseball player and ambassador for Major League Baseball in Pro Athletes Outreach*

cessfully doing something of my own choosing."[1]

Time and time again, I have met men who have very successfully done things of their own choosing, but they lacked the joy and contentment that come when a man lives in reckless abandon to God's script for his life rather than his own conclusive game plan.

A sport psychologist once shared with me that he had a sobering wake-up call at a men's conference. The Lord challenged him regarding the way he trained athletes to reach their goals through vicious perseverance—but gave no opportunity for God to compensate or even be acknowledged. Training men in the skill of stoicism for the sake of a gold medal leaves no room or need for God. After this epiphany, this life coach continues to train some of the best to reach Olympic goals, but now he encourages a healthy identity in Christ and giving God praise and glory for giving such great gifts to them.

Reckless Abandon = Passionate Followers of Christ

Unfortunately, because of our obsession with sex in the U.S., the word *passion* is usually assumed to be referring to sexual desire. In the not-so-distant past, though, *passion* referred to a person's relentless pursuit of his ideals and goals. I'm always shocked when people start to squirm in the presence of a passionate Christian, yet they don't flinch when someone is expressing boundless enthusiasm about a rock star or a winning sports team. One Sunday I came upon two verses that rocked my world: "For now we really live, since you are standing firm in the Lord. How can we thank God enough for you in return for all the joy we have in the presence of our God because of you?" (1 Thess. 3:8–9).

> I want a man who marries my daughter to be loving. If he has a love for God, it will transform his life. Love transforms a man's life and propels him through the storms and joys of life.
> —Drew Tucker Sr., pastor/ "sheepherder"

I was absolutely captivated by the phrase "really live." As I examined the words more closely, I discovered some of the synonyms were *vivifying, lively, intense*. Paul said that his life had taken on a more vivid, intense, and lively quality because of the passionate faith of the followers of Jesus in Thessalonica.

A Bozo will have reckless enthusiasm for man's accomplishments and worldly pursuits. A Boaz will be passionate about *God's* accomplishments through man and pursuits with eternal value.

A Passionate Christ-Follower: A Man of the Word

A Boaz actually knows where his Bible is and he doesn't use it as a coaster for a glass of iced tea. It has been said, "A Bible that is falling apart reflects a life that isn't." With that in mind, I would like to suggest that a Bible that hasn't even had its

The ultimate quality in an ideal man is that he is a man of prayer. He expresses his love and is passionate about life. He is a servant.

—Mike Singletary, NFL Hall of Famer, professional football coach

binding strained reflects a life that is more dependent on self than God.

While we don't know many details of Boaz's life, we do see that he knew, respected, and obeyed God's Law—therefore, he must have been a man of the Word. He must have studied its contents or listened to its being read. The fact that he followed his feeling that he should obey it and acted on it is what is most important.

My son-in-law noted, "Where do you look for your ideals as a man? I don't see how you can look anywhere before God's Word. I do not discount my experiences with other godly men and what I have read about great men in history, but I think when my experiences drive my perspective instead of God's Word, I run the risk of emulating a finite man when I should look like the infinite Savior."

King David was a poet warrior who was a champion in the Word. The psalms David wrote revealed that he was a king who kept the Word close to his side. Since I was a young Christian, he has shown me that men do have the capacity to spend time in God's Word, communing and meditating on it day and night. If a man can spend hours on the Internet "Googling," why can't he spend at least a few minutes a day reading the Word?

At a national football conference, I sat next to a pastor from Poland. This humble pastor was translating the Bible for the Poles by using copies of the Dead Sea Scrolls. Trust me, this was no small accomplishment! The pastor's investment of time is comparable to any training an athlete undergoes each season.

As we were chatting, he made an amusing remark to me: "I think God loves women better than He does men!" I asked him why he said such a thing, and he replied, "After a week with so many professional ballplayers, I think God gave men an ability to throw a ball, but he gave women the ability to sit at Jesus' feet and learn."

> An ideal man should be compassionate, surrendered to God and His will, and a passionate lover of God.
> —Whit, student at Dallas Theological Seminary

I chuckled, and then I thought about the amount of time, money, and energy men spend on games and sports magazines (boating, hunting, fishing, racing, etc.) and how they find it impossible to spend a few minutes a day reading God's Word.

Let's face it, girls: Boazes know what's important and they invest their time in it. Bozos don't care about discipleship, passion, or changing others' lives. They just want to win the video game!

The pastor from Poland was referring, of course, to the famous passage where Martha was angry that her sister, Mary, was sitting at Jesus' feet while Martha slaved away making dinner. When Martha complained about Mary to Jesus, His reply was for men and women alike: "'Martha, Martha,' the Lord answered, 'you are worried and upset about many things, but only one thing is needed. Mary has chosen what is better, and it will not be taken away from her'" (Luke 10:41–42).

A Boaz knows how to choose what is better. He knows that

to spend time reading God's Word is not just the requirement of a spiritual leader but the normal behavior for every follower of Jesus. Unfortunately, many followers of Jesus in the U.S. have a spiritual eating disorder. A man will never have enough stamina to live a life of reckless abandon without a consistent, daily, growing relationship with God through His Word.

A MWWF—God's Word in His Head and His Heart

You may stumble across a subtle version of a Bozo: the man who has head knowledge of Scripture but no heart connection to God. How can someone know the Word but not know God? It's the difference between knowledge and intimacy, rituals and relationship, and religion and Christianity. Furthermore, it is certainly the difference between a Bozo and a Boaz.

Such a man may attend church regularly. He may even participate in Bible studies or men's groups. Years ago, I was talking with my mentor, Bettye, about a man who knew so much of the Word of God but was an unloving bully. I asked, "How can this be?" She responded to my question by telling me a story she'd read years ago.

There was a little village church in Russia where attendance at Sunday school picked up after the minister started handing out candy to the children. One of the most faithful was a precocious lad who recited his Scriptures with proper devotion, pocketed his reward, and then ran into the field to munch on it. The minister took a liking to the boy and persuaded him to attend church school. The boy preferred doing this to household chores, so he went. By offering other rewards, the teacher managed to teach the boy *all the verses of the four Gospels.* He won a special prize for learning all Matthew, Mark, Luke, and John by heart and reciting them nonstop in a church service. Five decades later, he would recite Scriptures, but in a context that would horrify his old teacher. You see, the prized pupil who memorized so much of the Bible was Nikita Khrushchev, the late Communist premier.

This story illustrated how people can learn the Word but never know God intimately. It was also a reminder of the many ways a person can use the Word for his or her own agenda. If Nikita Khrushchev, a Communist dictator, could use the Word to make his points, I shouldn't be surprised when I see a person using God's Word to bully and manipulate other believers. Beware of the Khrushchev spirit—beware of the Bozos who can talk the talk but their behavior never measures up.

God's Word is not just for Sunday school boys to memorize, or a Communist premier to quote out of context. When President George W. Bush mentioned reading God's Word, many Christians were impressed. A key passage in the fifth book of the Old Testament teaches that a king is to have God's Word nearby at all times (as we saw with David). We need not be impressed when a president or a king or any celebrity reads God's Word; we should see it as a normal manifestation of a personal relationship with the Author.

> When he takes the throne of his kingdom, he is to write for himself on a scroll a copy of this law, taken from that of the priests, who are Levites. It is to be with him, and he is to read it all the days of his life so that he may learn to revere the LORD his God and follow carefully all the

> The ideal man is passionately in love with the Lord, full of wisdom granted from the Lord, and he tries to honor the Lord in all he does while keeping His commands.
> —Jonathan, barista

words of this law and these decrees and not consider himself better than his brothers and turn from the law to the right or to the left. (Deuteronomy 17:18–20)

Think of the irony of what some leaders keep in their top desk drawer. Instead of a copy of God's Word, too often it is something to "take the edge off" the pressure of leadership.

Men Who've Made Their Mark

I recently thought of two trios of men who have impacted the world we live in. The first trio includes Tiger Woods, Lance Armstrong, and Michael Jordan. Most people on this planet know who these three men are. Their stunning accomplishments in sports have made them household names.

The other trio has impacted the world, but they are not necessarily names we think of often. Aug, Lu, and Cal are my nicknames for Saint Augustine, Martin Luther, and John Calvin. These men are the Bravehearts of Christianity. They are leading warriors in the history of the battle for the souls of mankind, three men who influenced Christianity profoundly. They are all men who lived this verse: "Be on your guard; stand firm in the faith; be men of courage; be strong" (1 Cor. 16:13).

These men had a common characteristic: their lives were

changed by the Word of God. It always amazes me that a man can quote the statistics of a team's record but he can't quote one complete verse from the New Testament or even know who Aug, Cal, or Lu is.

I got to hear a modern Braveheart, author Erwin McManus, speak at a Pro Athletes Outreach Football Conference. After he finished speaking, everyone in the audience was given a book. I read the book the men were given first. It is a classic; I read it cover to cover on my flight home. The book was McManus's *The Barbarian Way*. Erwin is a Boaz, a man with a reckless abandon to pursue Jesus. Here is just one of the challenges this modern Braveheart shared in this book.

> A godly man possesses a confidence of who he is in Christ, an unquenchable thirst to know more of Christ, and a faith that is contagious.
> —Tim, self-employed, postal worker, basketball referee

To have the Spirit of God dwelling within the heart of someone who chooses a domesticated faith is like having a tiger trapped within a cage. You are not intended to be a spiritual zoo where people can look at God in you from a safe distance. You are a jungle where the Spirit roams wild and free in your life. You are the recipient of the God who cannot be tamed and a faith that must not be tamed. You are no longer a prisoner of time and space, but a citizen of the kingdom of God—a resident of the barbarian tribe. God is not a sedative that keeps you calm and under control by dulling your senses. He does quite the opposite. He awakens your spirit to be truly alive.[2]

After reading Erwin's book, I started thinking about other men who live with such reckless abandon: authors Rob Bell, Louie Giglio, Andy Stanley, Matt Redman, and Francis Chan, and singer Chris Tomlin. These men are making their mark on this generation. A Boaz is a man who not only makes his mark in his community but, through reckless abandon, impacts people beyond his small social realm.

My friend Renee, a "baseball wife" and mom of three boys, reflected on the importance of a man's total commitment to Jesus—she sums up so well some vital qualities of a godly man: "The first characteristic of the ideal man is dedication to the Lord so that he makes all decisions only after lining up with God's desires, even if that means big changes. [It also means] being honest at all times, even when it is not politically correct, and having a desire for knowledge from God's Word and the ability to stand firm in it."

A Man of Reckless Abandon Ends Up a Cooked Goose

When Ken and I visited Prague, we saw a statue of a man in the middle of the town square. I wondered aloud who he was, and Ken told me it was a statue of Jan Hus.

In the fifteenth century, Jan Hus, I later learned, spoke boldly against abuses and doctrinal errors in the Roman Catholic church, and because he refused to recant, he was burned at the stake. Just before Hus was put to death he said, "Today, you are burning a goose [the meaning of 'Hus' in Czech]; however, a hundred years from now, you will be able to hear a swan sing, you will not burn it, you will have to listen to him."[3]

One hundred years later, Martin Luther nailed his liberating Ninety-Five Theses to the Wittenberg door. Martin Luther saw himself as the fulfillment of Jan Hus's prophecy, and he accepted the symbol of the swan. What absolutely blew me away is that Hus worked to get the Bible into the language of the everyday man, and he was burned alive because of this effort. Before he was put to death, after much torture, he still had breath in him to prophesy about the coming liberation under Martin Luther (a hundred years later).

Where is the Jan Hus of the twenty-first century? When I think about his courage to live outside the box spiritually and stand courageously for what he believed, I have to conclude that a modern Boaz has to bravely swim upstream against the rushing stream full of Bozo guys. I am not expecting guys to step up and volunteer to be burned at the stake for what they believe! I just think that a great guy, a modern Boaz, will actually *know* what he believes and be able to articulate it if the occasion arises.

A MWWF, a man of reckless abandon, will be bold and affect many outside his small social circle. Just like Hus, Luther, Calvin, and Augustine.

Reckless Abandon: Hunger for God's Word

Just yesterday on the radio, a leader in family ministries in this country challenged listeners to turn off their TVs for one month. That may seem radical, but to even consider what one watches on a Saturday night in preparation for what one might receive Sunday morning at church is, unfortunately, equally radical. Reckless abandon impacts every aspect of a person's life, including his or her relationship with those things that entertain and distract from eternal focus.

> It astonishes me how many Christians watch the same banal, empty, silly, trivial, titillating, suggestive, immodest TV shows that most unbelievers watch—and then wonder why their spiritual lives are weak and their worship experience is shallow with no intensity. If you really want to hear the Word of God the way He means to be heard in truth and joy and power, turn off the television on Saturday night and read something true and great and beautiful and pure and honorable and excellent and worthy of praise (Phil. 4:8). Then watch your heart un-shrivel and begin to hunger for the word of God.[4]

TV has helped produce a famine for the Word of God across our nation. When I first read the book of the minor prophet Amos, I was totally captivated by his warning of a coming famine, not for bread and water but for the Word of God. At that moment in my life, I made a decision to invest time each day filling up the chambers of my soul with God's Word. Amos's prophecy even remarks that "the beautiful people" will be impacted by a thirst for God's Word:

> "The time is surely coming," says the Sovereign LORD, "when I will send a famine on the land—not a famine

of bread or water but of hearing the words of the LORD. People will stagger everywhere from sea to sea, searching for the word of the LORD, running here and going there, but they will not find it. Beautiful girls and fine young men will grow faint and weary, thirsting for the LORD's word." (Amos 8:11–13 NLT)

> An ideal godly man should have unwavering trust in God and His plan for us, compassion for his fellow man, and uncompromising belief that the example Jesus gave is the standard for all time.
> —Fred Cornett, financial advisor

National relief organizations send money and supplies to places in the world impacted by a food famine. I think we followers of Jesus need to be as concerned about the famine reflected in the souls of too many of God's children.

Ladies, a Boaz would be part of the famine relief team. He would have so much of God's Word stored in his soul that he could share freely with those beautiful girls and fine young men who are thirsting for the Lord's Word. Do you have enough of God's Word stored in your soul? Do you know how to get your soul filled up daily (Isa. 50:4)? How about the guy you like—how does he measure up?

Boazes are full of passion for God and for His desire that all men be saved. Boazes follow God despite others' doubts and criticism. Boazes consider full obedience to God worthy of any human price. Bozos are all about themselves: their desires, their entertainment, their goals in life. The choice is yours.

DISCUSSION QUESTIONS

- ❧ Do you consider yourself a person who is living in reckless abandon to Jesus? *Acts 20:24* If not, what keeps you from completely surrendering control of your life to Jesus? Do you think that reckless abandon will keep you from the guy you are interested in at this time?

- ❧ Are you hesitant for anyone to know about your spiritual journey? Do you think it is something private or something that should be shared freely with others? Are you concerned about offending a prospective boyfriend through your spiritual focus? *Matthew 10:32–33*

- ❧ Discuss the quote: "There is no lasting happiness, success, or fulfillment in life apart from a consistent, daily, growing relationship with Jesus through His Word." Have you found this to be true in your life? Discuss what most people think is the key to lasting happiness.

- ❧ Do you consider reading God's Word a religious duty or a soul's delight? *Psalm 119:165* Discuss why reading God's Word is too often seen as a duty, not a delight.

- ❧ Is a man's passion for God a major component in your Man Worth Waiting For? Do you think it makes a difference?

- ❧ Do you know a guy who knows the Word but seems to lack a true intimacy with God? Do you see clearly the difference between popular Christianese speech and experiential intimacy with Jesus? Discuss how the knowledge of God's Word is only life-changing when connected with growing intimacy with Jesus.

♣ 9

faithful though flawed

While reading John Piper's book *The Legacy of Sovereign Joy,* I came upon a captivating adjective. When describing three famous men who impacted the world for Christ, men who were equally famous for their weaknesses, John referred to them as "flawed."[1] I latched onto that word. Over the years I have often remarked that I am "perfectly forgiven but not perfect." I have said from the platform many times, "On my best day, I am still a sinner." That usually provokes a few chuckles but I am sincere. The adjective "flawed" struck me as accurate yet merciful.

The ideal man is not a flawless man. The only flawless man remained single and returned to heaven after a short three decades on this planet. Of course I am referring to Jesus; and the follower of Jesus is called to faithfulness, not flawlessness.

First and foremost, an ideal man has a heart after God. He is also gentle and disciplined.
—Linda Wells, college instructor

When I look at the life of Boaz, I don't see a flawless man but a man faithful to God. The ideal man lives with such humility that he is not afraid that his flaws may become apparent. Why? Because the ideal man is learning that God has called him to be faithful, not flawless.

Look at how Paul described it: "[Jesus said,] 'My gracious favor is all you need. My power works best in your weakness.' So now I am glad to boast about my weaknesses, so that the power of Christ may work through me" (2 Cor. 12:9–10 NLT).

King David: Faithful Though Flawed

As a new Christian reading the New Testament book of Acts, I was drawn to the term "man after God's heart" (13:22). Of course, we know God made the remark concerning King David, and right there and then I decided I wanted to be a person described the way David was. I hadn't read the Old Testament yet, so you can imagine how surprised I was, years later, to study the life of David and see his glaring flaws.

As a young Christian, I reasoned that God referred to David as "a man after His heart" because David loved God's Word, a love displayed in so many psalms that David wrote. For years, my conclusion was satisfying. Then, as I studied not only David's life but also the lives of those around him, I came to see that he committed such heinous sins that they were irreconcilable with the phrase "man after God's heart."

King David is notorious for his adultery with Bathsheba. Even if a person has never read the Bible, he or she knows the story of King David and his affair. The extramarital relationship between a famous king and a beautiful woman may not seem so horrible to some, but when you add the related crime that David committed—arranging for Bathsheba's husband to be killed in battle—the situation is scandalous.

> Where do you look for ideals as a man? Jesus and King David.
> —Chris, pastor and counselor

Let me explain. When King David schemed to have Bathsheba's husband killed, he was not killing a mere soldier. He was killing Uriah, a convert to the God of Israel. Uriah was a Hittite who took the Hebrew name meaning "The Lord Is My Light."[2] More than being a convert, Uriah was one of the select "mighty men" who were like a military inner circle of protection for King David (2 Sam. 23:39). So you see, David was arranging the death of a loyal friend and brother in battle. Making David's crime even more serious, Bathsheba was the daughter of another inner-circle friend, Eliam (2 Sam. 23:34).

The key to King David, though, is not his flaws, which were many, but his response to God in spite of his flaws. David's famous psalm of repentance, Psalm 51, silences any of David's accusers. In that passage we discover the key to a flawed man's faithfulness: he admitted when he had failed, and he continued to pursue the hope of Israel.

David's faithfulness to God despite his fallibility is what differentiated him from the king who preceded him. King Saul withdrew into self-absorbed depression whenever he failed

> Look for a man who loves and serves the Lord while having some plan of where he's going with his life.
>
> —Kathy Edwards, nurse

(1 Sam. 28:20, 23). The prophet Samuel gave clear direction for the behavior that is expected of men who are pursuing faithfulness regardless of their fallibility; Samuel told the Israelites not to pull away from God when they failed: "Do not be afraid. . . . You have done all this evil; yet do not turn away from the LORD, but serve the LORD with all your heart. Do not turn away after useless idols. They can do you no good, nor can they rescue you, because they are useless" (1 Sam. 12:20–21).

Saul did not listen. When King David, on the other hand, was rebuked by the prophet Nathan—"Why did you despise the word of the LORD by doing what is evil in his eyes?" (2 Sam. 12:9)—he submitted to the consequences of his sins, and he admitted that his greatest sin was ultimately against the God who had been so good to him.

Although David was absolutely flawed, when he is described in the New Testament, he is not referred to in relation to his flaws but in relation to his faithfulness.

I know a pastor who failed miserably in the area of sexual morality, but instead of repenting and changing his lifestyle, he quit the ministry and is now selling used cars. How different from the way King David responded to failure, which was to write psalms that have encouraged others to repent and find restoration and hope in God as he did. Another spiritual leader I have respected for years also failed morally, yet he not only repented, he sought counseling as well. As he grew past his failings, he has gone on to write some of the best books I have read. He always reminds me of King David.

One pastor fails and is selling used cars, another pastor fails, learns from his poor choices, and writes books to encourage others to persevere in spite of their flaws and failings. The key is not the absence of flaws but the presence of faithfulness amidst the flaws.

A Reality Check

Every man has his flaws. Remember, the difference between one flawed man and another is what the man does with his failures. Does he pursue God despite his flaws? Every Man Worth Waiting For will have his defects. Every Christian can ultimately be described as a flawed saint. But every MWWF will seek God's glory with his life despite all that.

We must clarify the flaws you can be expected to live with and the flaws that are deal-breakers in a relationship. When someone cuts you off in traffic and you don't exhibit a rude gesture or honk your horn, that is a noble response. Yet, generally overlooking instances of bad behavior is not necessarily a good practice in a dating relationship.

Let me explain. In a serious dating relationship, when you are trying to overlook a bad behavior your boyfriend repeats again and again, your response moves from ennobling into enabling. You are actually sanctioning his repeated bad choices. Rather than being the bigger person overlooking a wrong, you are actually a person who is encouraging bad behavior. So often a woman will overlook a serious character flaw in a man (such as lying, addiction to porn or alcohol, gambling, narcissism)

Being committed to the Lord is the most important characteristic . . . followed by humility and integrity. A godly man should walk with the Lord, having his own joy and guidance from Him; have the Lord's mind about his parents and his family; and have the Lord's wisdom on his finances and worldview.

—Barb Cash, wife, mother, and Bible study leader

and assume that he will change. This so-called loving response will galvanize the growth of a character flaw.

Women are constantly crying to me about the serious bad choices their husbands make. Those bad choices reflect significant character flaws that had manifested while these couples were dating, but the women overlooked them in the name of "love."

Girl, your boyfriend is showing you now whether he is a Bozo (with dangerous personality flaws) or a Boaz (flawed but passionate in his pursuit of God). Which is he?

A MWWF Measures Himself Fairly

You may be uncomfortable with the idea of being flawed. The gift we have been given in Jesus is stored in a very earthy container, as Paul pointed out: "But we have this treasure in jars of clay to show that this all-surpassing power is from God and not from us" (2 Cor. 4:7). What is so fabulous is that our flawed earthiness does not diminish the incomparable power of Jesus.

At a coaches' conference in Fort Lauderdale, I spotted a most amazing coach named Joe Erhmann while I was standing in line for the buffet dinner. I gingerly made my way up to him to introduce myself. I was a little enthusiastic upon extending my hand to greet him and exclaimed, "I can't believe I get to hear you teach in person! I so admire what God is doing through you in high school football." Joe's immediate response to me was: "Hi, I am just a struggling brother." Talk about deep humility! His response made him even more impressive to me.

> An ideal man relies on God and *does* what the Word says while being vulnerable and honest with his struggles and defects.
> —Linda Reed, single mom and conference planner

At that same conference, a former head baseball coach from the University of Kentucky spoke on the things he regretted from his twenty-eight years on the job. Instead of bragging about all he had accomplished as a coach, he admitted his shortcomings in front of a room full of coaches. I was absolutely blown away by his willingness to expose his flaws. This coach understood that every coach, even on his best game day, will fail and that a man teaches more effectively when he can be candid and transparent about the reality of daily struggles in the game of life.

Your Boaz will understand the same thing. Are you dating him now?

Pride Is Sin's Defense Attorney

Flawed servants are sensitive to the blinding power of pride. A mature Christian will not hide his flaws through pride's camouflage.

Let me explain. The pastor of a megachurch was caught in

an adulterous affair. When he sent a letter to every member of his church, the congregation assumed that he would express brokenhearted repentance. How stunned the members of the church were when they read a letter full of his *defense* of the affair! This flawed pastor allowed pride to be his defense attorney. His letter defending his sin stands in stark contrast to King David's psalm confessing his sin and begging God to restore their relationship.

My son-in-law, Drew, sent me an e-mail on this very topic. He wrote:

> Pride could also be called "practical atheism." Letting pride go on unaddressed in your heart is the life application of principles involved in atheism, is it not? It is out of pride that I often do not act in obedience to God's Word. Is it not ironic that believers "know" so much about what a life unto Christ is supposed to look like, but little obedience follows?
>
> It is hard to type stuff like this with a big log sticking out of my eye. I sit at a nice computer while people two miles from here cannot afford food. I will inevitably watch TV today though there is a country club across the street that I work at full of people destined for eternity apart from God . . . but I will watch TV instead of falling on my face before God and pleading for the salvation of those I work with and for.

This young man is a classic Boaz. He is faithfully following God, and he is utterly candid about his shortcomings. A Boaz is secure enough in his relationship with God and God's grace that he can be open about the areas that he needs to grow in. A Bozo will use pride to camouflage his insecurity, consequently distancing himself from God. The psalmist affirmed, "Though the LORD is great, he cares for the humble, but he keeps his distance from the proud" (Ps. 138:6 NLT).

> An ideal godly man should embody an *authentic* love for God that is real, fresh, and raw.
> —Tim Cash, chaplain for the Atlanta Braves

A Fabulous Guy, but on His Best Day . . . Still a Man

One of the biggest surprises for so many single women who wait for God's best and finally marry their modern Boazes is that they are shocked when they discover (even on their honeymoons) that they have married mere men. I tell women all the time, "My husband is a great guy, but he is a lousy god." When I look to my husband to be anything more than a faithful yet flawed man, I am setting myself up for disappointment.

When a woman wants her husband to be her source of love, joy, peace, etc., she puts immeasurable pressure on the husband. God never intended for a man to be everything a woman needed (or vice versa)—that is an idolatrous mentality that doesn't sit well with our heavenly Bridegroom. The more a woman discovers that Jesus is her Source, the more she removes such pressure from her husband.

A good friend of mine went to a professional counselor about her battle with depression. If you looked at this woman's life, you would ask, "How can you possibly be depressed?"

This woman has it *all*, but material possessions have not kept her from constantly struggling with a low-grade fever that runs through her soul.

Recently, my friend had an epiphany in the counselor's office. The counselor helped her to see that she wants life to be a "ten," but life outside the Garden of Eden is too often a "five." This woman's absurd expectations were fueling her constant bouts with depression.

Are you like my friend? Do you want your man to be a "ten"? If you can learn to expect your Boaz to be a "five" (not in any deal-breaker ways, of course) and he occasionally is an "eight," you will feel as though you have received a bonus!

In the bestselling book *Incompatibility: Still Grounds for a Great Marriage,* Chuck and Barb Snyder address this "ten" mentality in a "five" world:

> One of the greatest hindrances to a happy, successful, fulfilling marriage relationship is found in the word *expectations*. We bring into marriage so many preconceived ideas of what an ideal wife or husband should do. When our mate disappoints us and does not fulfill these expectations, little blocks of resentment over time start to build a wall between the partners.[3]

Talking with a young woman who just celebrated her first year of marriage, I was so impressed with her joy and success. I couldn't even comprehend such a great first year. My first year of marriage, though I was married to a classic Boaz, had so much heartache for me. Why? I had mentally constructed a list of expectations that no man could ever measure up to. I wanted my early years of marriage to be a "ten," but I did not take into account the "five" world we were living in. I kept forgetting that Ken and I did not move into the Garden of Paradise when we got married.

We are still living outside the garden in a very challenging world full of opportunities for disappointment and even disillusionment. I have heard it often said, "You can tell a lot about people's spiritual maturity by noting their response to chaos. Mature Christians have learned that life is more chaotic than predictable." Recognizing this reality will help any man or woman maneuver the rough waters of life.

Loving a flawed man for a lifetime requires that you understand the ebb and flow of love. Mature love understands that on some days, one's love is like high tide, and on other days, it's more like low tide. A flawed though faithful man will be a journey partner who is learning how to live unselfishly during the high and low tides of life.

Remember, your Boaz will allow you to continue in the direction of your life adventure designed by God. He will allow you to stay in your "lane" and finish the race you are in. He will be a lifelong dancing partner even if he knows he has two left feet.

Dreams Kept Safe

Some women confuse absurd *expectations* with *ideals*. They are not the same. The ideals that I write about in this book are taken from God's Word and God's standards for men and women. Expectations flow from what people think they deserve in a certain situation. Pride actually fuels our expectations. Pride is an overinflated view of what we deserve in life.

If you are a Ruth who is seeking a Boaz, you need to daily give your dreams and expectations to God for safekeeping. So much disappointment flows from what we expect and do not get—whether from an employer, parent, friend, mate, or even a child.

> *Every expectation,*
> *every plan,*
> *every dream*
> *not yielded to God,*
> *is a potential broken dream in the making.*
>
> —JMK

When I was a young Christian, I would always preface my dreams and plans with the phrase "If the Lord wills." Using that phrase reminded me to give my plans and dreams to God. "And now, Lord, what do I wait for? My hope [expectation] is in You" (Ps. 39:7 NKJV).

An older Christian once said to me, "You do not need to say 'If the Lord wills' to sound spiritual." I never thought of using the phrase as a way to sound spiritual. I used that phrase to remind myself who is ultimately in charge of my dreams. Sometime later, I realized that the phrases "If the Lord wills" or "Lord willing" are not only wonderful reminders for the one who uses those words, but also a reminder for anyone who hears them.

In the short book written by the brother of Jesus (James), we are encouraged to use the phrase "If the Lord wills." I think one of the reasons is to remind us to give our blueprints and dreams to the Lord for His authorization on a continual basis. James wrote: "Now listen, you who say, 'Today or tomorrow we will go to this or that city, spend a year there, carry on business and make money.' . . . Instead, you ought to say, 'If it is the Lord's will, we will live and do this or that.' As it is, you boast and brag. All boasting is evil" (James 4:13, 15–16).

A Flawed but Faithful Man Is Not Afraid of Powerlessness

Having several siblings who are substance addicts, I've learned that the first step in recovery from addiction is facing one's powerlessness. I am keenly aware of human pride and the resistance to admit weakness. A flawed though faithful man understands that admitting powerlessness leads him to the greatest power on earth—the power of prayer.

Martin Luther's last written words were, "We are beggars. This is true."[4] I love that remark, because one of the Greek words translated "pray" means "beg." The woman I pray with and I call ourselves "Beggar Partners." In the first gospel we find a verse that talks about "beggar partners": "Again, I tell you that if two of you on earth agree about anything you ask for, it will be done for you by my Father in heaven" (Matt. 18:19). Looking around me today, I have to ask: where are the Boaz men with the courage to be beggar partners rather than just golfing or fishing buddies?

A Boaz is a man with the courage to acknowledge his various needs and beg God for His gracious intervention/participation in his life. A man does not have to be an addict to admit his powerlessness; he just has to have the courage to look at himself with sober judgment.

Men are often inspired by the courage of a mighty warrior, hence the popularity of the big-screen hits like *Braveheart*, *Gladiator*, and *Master and Commander*. The nation of Israel had many famous warriors, but one who often comes to mind is Joshua. During a greatly successful military campaign, Joshua stood in front of all his men and did what I have never seen a mighty warrior do in the movies: he stopped and prayed.

> On the day the LORD gave the Amorites over to Israel,
> Joshua said to the LORD in the presence of Israel:
>> "O sun, stand still over Gibeon,
>>> O moon, over the Valley of Aijalon."
>> So the sun stood still,
>>> and the moon stopped. . . .
> There has never been a day like it before or since, a day
> when the LORD listened to a man. (Joshua 10:12–14)

I married a man who has his flaws; nevertheless, his ability to be a warrior in prayer has been a daily gift to me for more than three decades. On our first date, Ken asked if he could close our time in prayer, and he has been closing our days in prayer ever since that first warrior gesture. You don't need a man who will pray in front of the best fighting men on earth, but you need a man who is capable of praying in front of you and your little ones someday. You need a Boaz who can stop in the midst of chaos and consult the Lord, admit his powerlessness, and ask for God's intervention.

In our home, praying has always been like breathing. Praying is simply communication between two people who love each other. Our family has always prayed, because we are simply communicating together with the One who loves us more than we could ever love one another.

> The ideal man loves God and demonstrates this by his lifestyle.
>
> —*Susan Cornett, teacher*

A MWWF Is a Flawed Man Growing Spiritually

Spiritual growth is an ongoing adventure of trust. To God, trust is the ultimate barometer of a man's spiritual growth. How he handles the challenges in life reveals whether or not the concept of trust is a daily practice or an abstract concept.

While my youngest brother was in a Christian rehab center, he shared a principle that fortified his successfully overcoming his addiction. This principle is a classic picture of the struggle involved in the growth process: "If a man does not discover who he is in Christ, he will go back and uncover who he was apart from Christ, because the flesh always gravitates towards what is familiar and the Spirit gravitates towards what is unfamiliar."

The flawed-yet-faithful man grows as he discovers who he is in Christ. He is learning how to be motivated more by God's Spirit than the familiar nudges of his flesh—as the apostle Paul recommended: "So I advise you to live according to your new life in the Holy Spirit. Then you won't be doing what your sinful nature craves" (Gal. 5:16 NLT).

One of my favorite single guys at Dallas Seminary, Cody McQueen, captured the lack of trust that too many men display:

It is impossible to read through the Bible and not see men trusting God. The "Hall of Faith" in Hebrews 11 records men of the past who trusted in God for something they could not provide themselves. The psalms of King David are [full of] this same trust, no matter what the circumstances, no matter who the enemy.

Somehow we have missed this point as men today. We have grown up in a culture that offers the hope of the American dream and promotes the self-made man. We can name plenty of stories of men who have started from humble beginnings and now sit on executive boards as entrepreneurs and CEOs. Their strategies, however, are oftentimes much different from God's.

Contrary to popular belief, nowhere in the Bible does it say, "God helps those who help themselves." However, the Bible does say, "God humbles the proud and exalts the lowly." To make oneself low in the eyes of the world shows a lot of trust in God. It takes a lot of trust to be honest on your taxes, knowing God will provide, instead of being conniving and deceptive and using your own wits to finagle the numbers for certain gain. It takes a lot of trust to leave your child in the hands of the Lord and promote her God-given gifts instead of cramming her into the mold of the next successful doctor or lawyer you want her to be. It takes a lot of trust to quit your job because you feel your duties in your company compromise your integrity.

It is exactly this kind of trust that the Lord delights in, and it is exactly this kind of trust that brings life to a man's soul. To trust the Lord, to take risks for the sake of his name and your integrity, is an adventure. If you are bored (which is said of many men in our churches today), then step out and trust the Lord. He promises to give you all the adventure and breathtaking risks you can handle.

A MWWF Knows God's Love Language

Look at Psalm 16:3: "As for the saints who are in the land, they are the glorious ones in whom is all my delight." When was the last time you realized that you are capable of bringing God delight? As I spent time thinking about how I can delight God, I realized that what pleases God is my faith in Him. Hebrews 11:6 validates this conclusion: "Without faith it is impossible to please God." Faith, you might say, is God's love language.

Every challenging situation you and I face is an opportunity to love on the Lord. Every crisis that demands deep faith is a great time for loving on the Lord. If you are struggling with prolonged singleness, it, too, is a challenge of faith, another chance to love on the Lord. When another one of your friends gets married and you remain still single and dateless, this extreme challenge of faith is an enormous opportunity to love on your Lord!

If trust is not a strong trait in your life, take a red pen or pencil, read through the book of Psalms, and circle the word "trust" everywhere you find it. Let the many red circles be a reminder of God's love language and your constant opportunities to bring Him delight—to face the challenge of trusting God even when life seems so unfair.

A MWWF Is Not Ashamed of His Faith

For years I have enjoyed watching movies about historical heroes, men and women who were willing to risk their lives doing the most courageous things. Such brave souls are always an inspiration. What I find amazing is that men will charge into a bloody battlefield or into a burning building to rescue a child, but they nearly faint at the prospect of speaking freely about their faith. I have seen guys who will tell the most elaborate story for a huge crowd of people, but whenever asked about their faith, they stutter and stumble as if someone is holding a gun on them. I am so grateful for guys who are not ashamed of their faith. Boazes are flawed but faithful, and I have had the privilege of knowing Jesus intimately because I met some Boaz guys who weren't ashamed of their faith.

Recently in Atlanta, after the Marlins and the Braves played their scheduled game, a famous baseball pitcher named John Smoltz shared how he came to place his hope and trust in Jesus. You might think that when you are a famous baseball player, who plays before enormous crowds all the time, it is easier to share your faith. Not so. I have worked with professional athletes for fifteen years, and I know so many are totally unnerved at the thought of having to talk about their beliefs. I know men who can charge into a fierce line of football players yet can't charge the enemy of their faith by standing up for their God. I have seen fear melt the heart of a giant of a man.

A Boaz can't help but speak of his faith because it is his identity. A Bozo keeps such information to himself for fear of losing his identity.

On April 15, 1967, at a Bible study, a teenager named Larry

showed me how I could receive the gift of eternal life. I enthusiastically placed my faith in Jesus and accepted this free gift. After I left the Bible study, I hurried home to call my best friend, Judy. When she answered the phone, I began to tell her how she, too, could receive the gift of eternal life through Jesus Christ. Her response: "Oh, I already did that when I was in elementary school."

Confused, I said, "I am probably not explaining this clearly. I asked Jesus Christ to come into my heart today, and I know I am going to heaven."

Judy answered in an aggravated voice, "Jackie, I told you I already asked Jesus into my heart when I was at a church camp."

I said, "There is no way you'd have such great news and not share it with me. We've been best friends for two years!"

We started to argue. I kept repeating how shocked I was that my best friend could keep secret something so significant as *knowing how to get to heaven*. For many years, I have met Christians like my best friend who are comfortable keeping this good news to themselves. I have always felt it was a crime to keep such information from those who need it. "We're not doing right. This is a day of good news and we are keeping it to ourselves" (2 Kings 7:9).

A Boaz doesn't have to stand on street corners waving at cars and shouting about Jesus. A Boaz doesn't have to go door to door telling people how to get to heaven. A man who has learned to be faithful though flawed will be transparent enough to share his journey with other people when asked about his hope amidst his flaws.

The Flawed Man Grows More Faithful— How You Can Tell

Speed-dating doesn't allow you to observe the spiritual growth of another person. But friendship with the opposite sex does— it allows you to see not only the direction of the man's life but also his values and morals and spiritual growth over time.

How often have you heard people say, "A person's religion is a private matter"? Well, something as wonderful as a personal relationship with the Creator of the universe cannot be kept quiet. Does a newly engaged girl wear gloves to hide her engagement ring? A Boaz doesn't hide his love for the God who saved him!

A dear friend was telling me about a speaking opportunity her husband had. He titled his message for the men's group: "From Jock to Jerk to Jesus." I burst out laughing when I heard the title. His message was clearly one about the spiritual growth of a flawed, faithful man. This flawed man has helped raise three of the finest children I have known. They knew their dad wasn't perfect, but his flaws were framed in faithfulness to God, wife, and family. This man lived the truth of Scripture: "Now it is required that those who have been given a trust must prove faithful" (1 Cor. 4:2).

It should comfort you to know that flawed men can still be faithful men; that even a Boaz has his off days and moments. This means you don't have to be flawless either! You're not looking for Mr. Perfect. You're looking for Mr. Right, and he will be a man who maintains his faith despite his flaws.

DISCUSSION QUESTIONS

- ✿ Discuss the statement: "God has called us not to flawlessness but to faithfulness." *Psalm 51:10–13* Is this quote comforting or confusing to you? Explain.

- ✿ Have you learned to be faithful even though you're aware of your own flaws? Do you fear having to admit your flaws? Why?

- ✿ Do you think that being a Christian means you must have a flawless image? *1 Samuel 12:20–21*

- ✿ Do you tend to have absurd expectations of others? Do you want life to be a "ten" when outside the garden it will often be a "five"?

- ✿ Have you ever seen someone harm a good relationship through unrealistic expectations?

- ✿ A Man Worth Waiting For is faithful though flawed: does that sound like a contradiction to you? Explain.

- ✿ Discuss what a flawed man growing more faithful looks like.

✿ 10

surrounded by good company

While doing research for a message on "The Divine Se-
crets of the Yada Yada Sisterhood," I came across the
Hebrew word *yad*. This word is found in a passage referring to
Jonathan's going out to find his friend (future King David) in
the wilderness to encourage him as he faced the battle of his
life. The battle wasn't against the giant Goliath but a bigger
"giant," a jealous king named Saul—Jonathan's father.

We see this recorded in 1 Samuel: "While David was at
Horesh in the Desert of Ziph, he learned that Saul had come
out to take his life. And Saul's son Jonathan went to David
at Horesh and helped him find strength in God" (23:15–16).
The phrase "helped him find strength" captures the definition
of the Hebrew word *yad*. Jonathan is what I would call a *Yad
Brother*—someone who strengthens others in crisis.

David's son Solomon would one day write about the comfort a Yad Brother can be during a life challenge. Solomon probably heard stories about the help his father received in battle from Prince Jonathan. I wonder if the stories were a frame for this verse Solomon wrote: "If one falls down his friend can help him up. But pity the man who falls and has no one to help him up!" (Eccl. 4:10).

A Boaz keeps himself surrounded by good company. A Bozo prefers the company of other Bozos.

Duties of a Yad Brother

The phrase "helped him find strength" refers to speaking words that give internal encouragement to remain strong. I would love to have heard what Jonathan said to David, when you consider that the one seeking to kill David was Jonathan's father. Talk about an emotional crisis!

Jonathan was a prince who was exceptional in friendship and loyalty. What a contrast he was to Amnon's friend Jonadab, who encouraged Amnon to take what he wanted and satisfy his lust-filled cravings. Ultimately, that "encouragement" helped defeat Amnon and led to his death. Jonathan, on the other hand, helped his friend succeed—and live.

Reading how Jonathan encouraged David, I declared one day that Jonathan was the official leader of the Yad Band of Brothers. Remember the scene in the movie *Braveheart* where the ragtag team from Ireland arrives in the woods to pledge its allegiance to William Wallace? This crew of courageous men was committed to encouraging William Wallace to continue his leadership.

In the first century, when one of the greatest Christians was struggling, God sent a Yad Brother to help him find strength in the battle of life—rescuing souls from societal insanity. Paul wrote, "For when we came into Macedonia, this body of ours had no rest, but we were harassed at every turn—conflicts on the outside, fears within. But God, who comforts the downcast, comforted us by the coming of Titus" (2 Cor. 7:5–6). Here we have Paul admitting the external and internal stress he and his band of brothers were facing, and God sent comfort through another brother. Whether it was Jonathan sent to David in battle or Titus sent to Paul in the battle for souls, both men came bearing words of encouragement.

Again, Boazes keep good company—people who encourage.

A Yad Brother's Verbal Ministry

Both Jonathan and Titus exercised the life-giving power of wise and helpful words. An Old Testament prophet was given the difficult job of guiding and exhorting a dreadfully stubborn king. The prophet's name was Samuel, and the Bible describes him most favorably: "As Samuel grew up, the LORD was with him, and everything Samuel said was wise and helpful" (1 Sam. 3:19 NLT).

Seven powerful words: "Everything Samuel said was wise and helpful." What made Samuel's words so effective in helping people? The key to his communication appears in a previous verse, where Samuel answered the call of God by saying, "Speak, LORD, for your servant is listening" (1 Sam. 3:9). In Hebrew, "listening" is *sama*—"undivided attention."

The Scripture states that the prophet Samuel never spoke

useless, meaningless words. The New International Version puts 1 Samuel 3:19 this way: "The LORD was with Samuel as he grew up, and he let none of his words fall to the ground." What is usually on the ground? Rotting vegetation, roadkill, and trash, among other things. What words might we find lying on the ground, figuratively speaking? What words belong in the trash rather than in a gift package sent to a Yad Brother in battle?

Paul answered this: "Do not let any unwholesome talk come out of your mouths, but only what is helpful for building others up according to their needs, that it may benefit those who listen" (Eph. 4:29). "Unwholesome talk" in this verse refers to rot/decay. If we are to avoid "unwholesome" words pouring out of our mouths, we need to give the Lord "undivided attention." I used to say of my son: "If I don't have his eyes [looking at mine], I don't have his ears." If our eyes are not focused on the truth of God's Word, we will be vulnerable to rushing to say things that are not beneficial to those who are listening.

Does the guy you like speak words that delight the recipients? Are his words a gift to the listener? Do his words build up or tear down? The Hebrew word translated "fall" refers to being brought down in a violent fall. For years I have heard youth leaders use Ephesians 4:29 to keep teens from swearing when the leaders could have challenged teens to consider that their conversations have the power to be a gift or roadkill rot.

How fascinated I would have been to have overheard the encouraging conversation between Prince Jonathan and David in the wilderness. So often men spend time together and never speak words of encouragement. How often are men together and, while they can share a thousand statistics about the stock

> have been most influenced by other men who have poured [themselves] into my life, especially in [showing me] how they handled their wives and kids.
> —David Faison, CLU, chartered financial consultant, Northwestern Mutual

market or the batting average of a favorite baseball player, they can't muster up one sentence of life-changing exhortation to a Yad Brother in need.

I remember when a man spent a weekend hunting with a friend whose marriage was on the brink of disaster, and this man never said one word of encouragement or even concern to his hunting buddy. His words may not have fallen to the ground as rotten fruit, but he certainly did not offer a piece of ripe fruit to nourish his friend's soul.

Yad Brothers Encouragement Manual

What does a Yad Brother use to find wise helpful words to help a brother in one of life's battles? Throughout the book of Acts, we read that Paul the apostle went around encouraging fellow believers. What guidebook did this Yad Brother use? The Word of God. Look at what Paul wrote about the Scriptures: "For everything that was written in the past was written to teach us, so that through endurance and the encouragement of the Scriptures we might have hope" (Rom. 15:4).

I looked up the Greek word translated "encouragement" and it was *paraklesis*. All of Scripture is actually a *paraklesis*—encouragement for the purpose of strengthening and establishing a believer in his faith. I have spent years harping (holy goading) on fellow believers to read their Bibles. To read one's Bible is to read an encouragement manual.

Recently one of my favorite Yad Brothers, Ed Flanagan, wrote to cheer up my sad and weary heart. Ed's e-mail referred to a verse I didn't recognize. When I looked it up, it so touched my heart that tears began to flow and the joy of the Lord began to fill my exhausted heart: "God is not unjust; he will not forget your work and the love you have shown him as you have helped his people and continue to help them" (Heb. 6:10).

> My influences include my wife, Liz, my mother, Annie Jane, and the godly men in my accountability group.
> —George Toles, marketing expert and former NBA broadcaster

Yesterday, a wonderful Yad Brother called me, and when I got off the phone, I was so excited that I was almost dangerous! I kept thinking about the verse he shared with me and how he was living its truth: "And let us consider how we may spur one another on toward love and good deeds" (Heb. 10:24).

All of us are called to encourage outbursts of love and good deeds in one another. We are each commissioned to be "holy spurs." Just as the spurs on a rider's boots urge the horse forward, so we are to urge one another forward on the race we are running toward Jesus. When you read your Bible daily, it is "spur polishing time." First God "spurs" you ahead and then you spur others onward in their journeys into the heart of God.

Yad Brothers (Men Worth Waiting For) know the Encouragement Manual. They know what words will strengthen an-

> If I were a man, I would seek out mentors I admired and plug in!
>
> —Linda Reed, single mom and conference planner

other brother, and they use their words as gifts. After a Yad Band of Brothers has spent time together, having been spurred on by one another, they will move back into their lives to continue loving others authentically through their faithful though flawed lives.

Yad Brothers and Community

We read Solomon's admonition in Proverbs: "Plans succeed through good counsel; don't go to war without advice of others" (20:18 NLT). In small groups, men discover the significance and enormous benefit of community. Too often a man is bogged down with doubts about his capacity to follow Jesus as he knows he should. In community, such a brother can discover that he is not alone in his struggles to be a faithful though flawed man. In other words, Men Worth Waiting For help each other stay strong.

Consider this reality: Paul challenged a group of Christians to follow him as he was following Jesus (1 Cor. 11:1). He did not say this to the strongest group of Christians he knew. Instead, he sent this challenge to a group of struggling believers living in the sin capital of the area. In community, the Band of Yad Brothers will reinforce the reality that a man can be faithful to Jesus even though he is truly flawed.

Boaz from Texas: Men Need Each Other

When I considered the framework and content of this book, there were some key guys I so wanted input from. One of these guys was Cody. He is one of those unforgettable people whose passionate pursuit of Jesus is so real and so raw. He is a certified member of the Yad Band of Brothers. In his comments on community, he captured the Yad Band of Brothers principle:

"No man is an island," and neither is any Christian. As Christians we were made for each other. We all have different needs and abilities, so we all fit together to make one functioning unit. We are not meant to carry our burdens alone but to cast them upon the Lord and confess our sins to one another ["Therefore, confess your sins to one another and pray for one another, that you may be healed"—James 5:16 ESV]. If you thought you were meant to be a Lone Ranger, you are sadly mistaken.

There is a community life of the Christian—one of fellowship, sharpening, and serving—that each of us must be a part of. We must be willing to rub up against one another if we are ever going to be changed into the people God wants us to be. Did you know that a washing machine gets clothes clean because the clothes rub up against each other? Clothes become clean with a little bit of soap and a lot of rubbing against each other.

The Lord has put us in this washing machine called the world and given us the one thing that can make us clean: the Holy Spirit. It is only when we interact with each other and the Holy Spirit that any sort of cleanliness can occur. Sometimes we get rubbed the wrong way by people and we feel that they are rude or inconsiderate, but that is only revealing how dirty we are and how clean we need to become. "As iron sharpens iron, so one man sharpens another" (Prov. 27:17).

Yad Band of Brothers Community Activity

Men's small groups offer deep discipleship as well as accountability. In these groups, men ask penetrating and important questions of one another:

- ✤ Have your words and actions displayed Jesus this week?
- ✤ Have you allowed your mind to entertain sexual thoughts about another?
- ✤ Have you given in to an addictive behavior this past week?
- ✤ Have you been honoring your key relationships this week (with wife/children/friends)?
- ✤ Have you offended another person by your words?
- ✤ Have you continued to remain angry toward another?
- ✤ Have you coveted something that does not belong to you?
- ✤ Have you been completely honest with us?

These questions are a glimpse of the honesty necessary for genuine accountability. With only shallow questions and sharing, a man can hang with the brothers for weeks and never expose a sin that may have captured his heart, a sin that could threaten his testimony, his marriage, or his livelihood. A Man Worth Waiting For has men around him who challenge him to be an authentic follower of Jesus.

It's disturbing but true: a man can be in a Bible study with other men and escape accountability for major sin problems. One man I know was actually leading a group of men through the book *Experiencing God,* yet because those brothers never asked hard questions, this Bible study leader continued to feed a secret sexual addiction. He could meet weekly with godly men and talk about experiencing God while he was experiencing the god of lust and not the God of heaven.

So many men are hesitant to ask these hard questions in order not to offend others, yet the greatest offense is to handle a person so superficially that he can be dying spiritually from a serious addiction with the men around him doing nothing to help him escape. The writer of Hebrews said, "But encourage one another daily, as long as it is called Today, so that none of you may be hardened by sin's deceitfulness" (Heb. 3:13).

Daily, sin is crouching at the door of a man's heart; how wise is the man who doesn't open it and how great the band of brothers who will help one keep the door closed. We see in Proverbs: "He who walks with the wise grows wise, but a companion of fools suffers harm" (13:20); "He who conceals his sins does not prosper, but whoever confesses and renounces them finds mercy" (28:13).

When a man is willing to operate in community, to be accountable to men he admires, he will grow close enough to his Yad Brothers that his struggles will not remain hidden. He will become a Boaz! Exposing one's struggles in a safe community of Yad Brothers is the frame for freedom from sin's captivating seduction. There is harm to be suffered in secrecy and there is liberty for men who have brothers to reveal their hearts.

My son-in-law, Drew, made these remarks about groups like the Yad Brothers:

I think biblical community is central to becoming more like Jesus: being involved in a local body of Christ and within that body being involved with guys who are grossly honest with one another. So, the top qualities are:

- ✿ Honest: with his wife and those men who are committed to his sanctification. John Piper says sanctification is a "community project." Without complete disclosure to those who are committed to your righteousness, growth cannot happen.

- ✿ Repentant: one who repents often of sin . . . which is often brought into the light because of the biblical community he is experiencing.

- ✿ Passionate: one who lives from the heart/soul; one who is passionate about eternal things.

- ✿ Committed to the body of Christ.

- ✿ Fruitful: one who is bearing fruit . . . often as a result of the above.

Faithful Wounds of a Yad Brother

A young man I know (I'll call him Justin) is in a small group where men ask each other hard questions. These are Boazes and Boazes-in-training! This accountability group is one of the best gifts this man can give his marriage and ministry. Proverbs says, "Better is open rebuke than hidden love. Wounds from a friend can be trusted, but any enemy multiplies kisses" (Prov. 27:5–6).

One week while the guys were listening to Justin's replay of the previous week's activities, a trusted friend challenged him, saying, "I hear that you are doing well at work and at school and at playing golf. But I don't think you are doing as well at loving your new bride." Ouch, but what a wonderful remark to guide a young newlywed. His friend also said, "Justin, I'm also good in seminary and great at playing basketball with the guys, but I don't do as well at loving my wife. That's the only reason I can see this need in you—I battle it in my own life."

Here again is proof of the existence of Men Worth Waiting For on Planet Earth in the twenty-first century. These guys are faithful though flawed and are committed as a Yad Band of Brothers to make a difference not only in the world, but at home in their marriages.

A real Boaz—a Yad Brother—not only seeks the truth about himself and others, he tells it. One time I asked a man why, when he played golf with his good friend, he did not discuss the struggles in his friend's marriage. He replied, "I have been a fan of his since high school, so I am too in awe of him to ask hard questions."

Wrong answer. To be in awe of another is too often idolatry, and sadly, this idolatrous gaze will silence the bravest of men. How distressing to think that such admiration would not become instead the faithful wound of a friend, which is more valuable than the flattery of an enemy.

Years ago, author Dr. Henry Brandt shared with me the number-one reason people do not speak openly with one another: "We don't want to face their anger and defensiveness when we wound them with the truth." A MWWF has the courage to endure the anger of a friend, until the friend finally comes to his senses. When the friend finally sees the error of his choices, he will be the most grateful to the one who had the courage to confront him. Too many friends stick to flattery as a loved one's life unravels from sin.

A Formidable Band of Yad Brothers

When God allowed Daniel and his friends to be taken away from their families and transported to the Babylonian palace, He created a formidable Yad Band of Brothers, which would ultimately impact all of Babylon. We know Daniel's friends as Shadrach, Meshach, and Abednego, the names they were given in captivity in Babylon. Their not-so-famous Hebrew names were Hananiah, Mishael, and Azariah. As I studied the Hebrew translations and meanings of these names, I discovered what kind of friends Daniel had, the kind we all need: friends who want passionately to follow God.

> *Hananiah* means "The Lord is gracious."
> *Mishael* means "Who is like our God?"
> *Azariah* means "The Lord is my help."[1]

Their very names held the messages those friends needed to give one another when all three were cast into the fiery furnace (Dan. 3). Their names described the gracious, incomparable, helping God who showed up in the furnace as the fourth man. The Lord, who walked in the fiery furnace with them, was the embodiment of all three of their names!

A MWWF has friends who remind him that the Lord is gracious, that He is their helper, and that He is an incomparable God. Yad Brothers/MWWF know how vital it is to remind others of God's gracious, incomparable help—especially those who are about to go into a fiery trial. Your closest friends are like a walking promo of your heart. As you associate you become. "Do two walk together unless they have agreed to do so?" (Amos 3:3).

> I look for my ideals as a man in the Word and hang with other men who are Jesus freaks!
> —Tim Cash, chaplain for the Atlanta Braves

Consider the people your guy spends the most time with—is he becoming like them? Do you see their behaviors and attitudes—good or bad—showing up in his life? Does the guy you like or love have friends like Daniel's? If not . . . he may be a Bozo. Watch out.

Yad Brothers Don't Snore During Others' Agony

We read of Jesus:

> He took Peter and Zebedee's two sons, James and John, and he began to be filled with anguish and deep distress. He told them, "My soul is crushed with grief to the point of death. Stay here and watch with me." He went on a little farther and fell face down on the ground, praying, "My Father! If it is possible, let this cup of suffering be taken away from me. Yet I want your will, not mine." Then he returned to the disciples and found them asleep. (Matthew 26:37–40 NLT)

There was Jesus in the press of pain, and His three inner-circle friends, Peter, James, and John, were snoring through His agony, even after Jesus had told them about what He was experiencing. Three best friends sleeping through a friend's pain—a tragic reality, I realized, but then I read a passage that recorded another incomprehensible response from the same inner circle of guy friends:

> Jesus took Peter, James, and John to a mountain to pray. And as he was praying, the appearance of his face changed, and his clothing became dazzling white. Then two men, Moses and Elijah, appeared and began talking with Jesus. They were glorious to see. And they were speaking of how he was about to fulfill God's plan by dying in Jerusalem.
>
> Peter and the others were very drowsy and had fallen asleep. Now they woke up and saw Jesus' glory and the two men standing with Him. (Luke 9:28–32 NLT)

This time they were dozing during the Transfiguration. They were dozing during a pep talk that Moses and Elijah were giving Jesus prior to His crucifixion. Best friends sleeping through both the glory and agony in the life of Jesus—what a miracle the Holy Spirit performed when He was sent to fill these men after the resurrection of Jesus. You might say they were Boazes-in-training while Jesus lived among them, and then through the Holy Spirit they became true Boazes after Jesus' death.

Let's look at a modern-day example. Christmas Eve 2004, a little boy was injured when his grandmother accidentally ran over him when backing out of the boy's parents' driveway. As the family rushed the boy to the hospital, the child's daddy called the leader of his Yad Band of Brothers.

In that emergency room on Christmas Eve, a Yad Band of Brothers watched, wept, and prayed over their grieving brother.

The death of this only son was an oil press of agony, but the Yad Band of Brothers helped to support the brother during his unimaginable loss. These men did not snore through this tragedy.

In the Garden of Gethsemane, Peter, James, and John missed a critical moment to be Yad Brothers to Jesus. On Christmas Eve, in the emergency room in Atlanta, a ragamuffin band of Yad Brothers made all the difference in the world to the life of a brother going through life's greatest agony—the loss of a child.

A Boaz surrounds himself with good people, and they comfort each other.

Sports and the Yad Band of Brothers

For fifteen years, I have taught and counseled professional baseball and football players and their wives through the national ministry of Pro Athletes Outreach. In my work with professional athletes, I have observed that sports give athletes more than celebrity status, big contracts, and glory; there is a camaraderie that makes for incredible teamwork on the field. Now sometimes this camaraderie creates the most supportive and valuable kind of community a guy could hope for. Other times, this same teamwork that can win championships on the field doesn't benefit the player off the field at all; it does little or nothing to encourage him to win in the game of life.

From the accounts of all types of athletes I have known, young and old, rookie and retired, baseball and football, this type of brotherhood in its best forms is the thing they most miss during their off-season and after retirement. It is not the roar of the crowd or the thrill of the game they long for, it is the

In the positive sense, Christ has influenced me the most, but [so have] the men in my life who live out Christ in their lives and set the example for me.
—*Eddie Taubensee, retired baseball player and ambassador for Major League Baseball in Pro Athletes Outreach*

fellowship with their guys. There is a compelling attachment to relationships that are meaningful for these men—all the more evidence that our Boaz brothers need to band together.

We've seen it again and again in this chapter. A MWWF is a Yad Brother: one who surrounds himself with wise friends, who accepts and gives strength, who respects the faithful wounds of a friend, and who is better for the company he keeps. Don't settle for anything less. If you don't like your guy's friends, beware: before long you won't like your guy either.

DISCUSSION QUESTIONS

- ❧ Does the Yad Band of Brothers exist in the twenty-first century? *1 Samuel 23:15–16* Do you know anyone who is part of such camaraderie? Describe him and his group.
- ❧ Do you see the inherent vulnerability of a man living in isolation from any community? *Hebrews 3:13, 10:25*
- ❧ Does this concept of a formidable band of brothers seem like another unrealistic ideal? Why?
- ❧ Are you part of a band of sisters who cheer you on in waiting for God's best? *Proverbs 13:20; 2 Corinthians 7:5–6; 1 Corinthians 7:33–34*

✿ Does the guy you like have friends like Daniel in his life? Can you think of specific friends whose actions remind you of these names?

> *Hananiah* means "The Lord is gracious."
> *Mishael* means "Who is like our God?"
> *Azariah* means "The Lord is my help."

✿ Are you well versed in the Encouragement Manual for the band of brothers or sisters? *Romans 15:4; Hebrews 10:24* Read and discuss these verses.

part III

your role in locating a MWWF

In the first two sections of this book, we've taken a thorough and honest look at Boazes, Bozos, and how to distinguish between the two. Finally we're ready to look at what *you* can do as you await the Man Worth Waiting For—how you can become a Ruth to whom a Boaz will be attracted!

don't be bozo bait

In this chapter, I'll explain how you can avoid being Bozo Bait—or even worse, a Bozo Magnet—by making smart decisions about your lifestyle. After all, if you want to attract a Man Worth Waiting For, you need to be a Woman Worth Waiting For. Following are some warnings to live, date, and love by.

Beware of a "Damaged Goods" Mentality

Faced repeatedly with the mystery of watching a fabulous woman settle for a Bozo guy, I have tried to understand what's happening. I know that it is not an unusual scenario, but there has to be a common thread that ties these women together in this sad yet predictable life choice. After years of study, I have come to believe that women settle for Bozos often because *they don't think they're worth the men of their dreams.* They see themselves as damaged goods. Let me illustrate this common distortion with a very personal example.

As I stood on the platform as the matron of honor for a precious young friend I had mentored for several years, Christina, a most painful thing occurred. As her bridegroom began to say his vows, he began to weep, as did his best man. I did not cry, I sobbed. The groom and his best man wept for joy. I may have begun crying for that reason, but the tears of joy turned to painful sobbing after the Father of Lies whispered, "Your bridegroom did not weep from joy for you, because you were damaged goods."

That one lie turned into hundreds of thoughts that spiraled around my mind. God gave Christina a wonderful Christian home to grow up in, with two loving parents and two great brothers. She grew up in a home where laughter and music were commonplace. I, in contrast, grew up in a non-Christian, abusive home, where screaming, fighting, and verbal abuse were the "music" I heard daily. I had not been given the blessings that Christina had, so yes, I was "damaged goods" on my wedding day.

But the day after Christina's wedding, Jesus showed me that my heavenly Bridegroom has wept for me. He wept in the Garden of Gethsemane and bravely faced the cross because of the joy that was set before Him—the joy of offering me forgiveness and taking me as His bride. He even gave me the Holy Spirit as His engagement ring (Eph.1:13–14). Jesus is actually madly in love with me and you (Eph. 3:17–19)! I realized that I had a choice to make: believe Jesus or the Father of Lies (John 8:44).

You may wonder how I could believe a lie when I am a follower of the truth, when I have the Spirit of truth within me (John 15:26). Let me explain. I daily have the choice to believe the truth or to exchange the truth for a lie. I have the choice to wound myself through lies or be healed through truths.

Adam and Eve were in a perfect relationship with God Almighty, but that perfect relationship did not keep Eve from believing a lie. We must recognize that as Christians we are following the truth, studying the truth, and living the truth, but that does not immunize us against being exposed to and even believing lies. We have a legacy of lies, because we were originally followers of the Father of Lies.

The "damaged goods" mentality is one of the enemy's favorite strategies to persuade God's girls to settle for Bozos rather than wait for Boazes.

Beware of Being a Bozo Magnet

On the *Today* show one morning, an English musician named Natasha Bedingfield was performing in Rockefeller Plaza. This pop star from Europe sang a song that had me cheering because the lyrics reaffirmed a powerful truth: women don't need men to validate them. I was thrilled that a beautiful single girl was declaring on national TV that a man was not the basis of her self-worth, for, as I have seen countless times, the surest way for a woman to end up a Bozo Magnet is the misbelief that a woman's value comes in direct proportion to the admiration she gets from a man.

What, you may be asking, is the difference between Bozo Bait and a Bozo Magnet? Women who are Bozo Bait have generally low standards of purity and passion for God. They draw the interests of men who are equally distracted from the things of God. Bozo Magnets are more developed models of Bozo Bait: they have so abandoned their ideals and pursuit of God that they actually look for and attract *only* Bozos. These women even set up long-term relationships with Bozos!

Author Dr. Leslie Parrott spoke at a 2002 conference about the need for women to find their identity and wholeness in one place alone—and the disastrous consequences that result when they don't: "If you try to build intimacy with another person before you have done the hard work of becoming whole on your own in Jesus, then all of your relationships become an attempt to complete yourself, and it sets you up for failure."

This comment parallels what Natasha was singing, but Dr. Parrott added a critical truth: a person with a "compulsion for completion" is not satisfied by a mere declaration of independence; she is finally satisfied only when she becomes whole on her own in Jesus. Natasha's declaration of independence from a man's validation is great, but if that includes a declaration of independence from God's love and validation, that is a road that will lead a woman into something even more painful than being a Bozo Magnet. That form of declaration of independence—from God—began with our foremother, Eve, and we all know where that led!

So many single women think that feeling incomplete comes from lack of a spouse rather than a lack of Jesus. In the process of total surrender to Jesus, a woman will discover that she can become whole—in Him she is complete. When two incomplete singles get married, their union will not make them complete. Their marriage will be simply two incomplete people trying to find completeness in one another. Only when they understand that their fullness is found in a relationship with Jesus will they be free to complement one another.

You were not created to *complete* another, but to *complement* another (no matter what Jerry Maguire said). Completion is Jesus' responsibility, and complementing is a woman's privilege. A woman not complete in Jesus will constantly be trying to get from her husband what only God can provide. She will expect her husband to fill the gap that only Jesus can fill—as I expected Ken to fulfill all my needs when we were first married. The single woman who has grasped the principle of becoming whole on her own in Jesus will be content even when there are no prospective guys on the horizon of her life. And she will be a *Boaz* Magnet, not a Bozo Magnet!

A woman can become a Bozo Magnet when she is not aware of her love hunger, which is exposed through her compulsion for completion. A woman needs to take the time to evaluate the condition of her "love tank." What does that mean? She needs to examine the family she grew up in. Did she feel loved by both parents and the rest of her family? Or did she grow up with a longing for love where she found herself looking for love in all the wrong places at a young age? A girl's empty love tank will create a hunger that drives her into boy-craziness at a young age.

I was never treated with honor by my father or my brothers; consequently, I had an insatiable appetite for love and attention from males. My love tank was definitely running on empty throughout my teens. But when I was born again, Jesus began to fill my love tank. Through His Love Letter to my heart (the Bible) and love from various members of His forever family, I began to experience love in the most compensating way. My love tank began to fill, and I wasn't as vulnerable to Bozo guys. You can experience this too. Your consistent, daily, growing relationship with Jesus through studying the Word is a sure love-tank-filler (Ps. 119:165).

Beware of Letting Sex Blur Your Vision

What could possibly keep a woman from seeing clearly the Bozo qualities in the guy she is dating? I have already covered this in detail, but let me reiterate here: the number-one thing that blurs a heart's vision is premarital sex. God wants us to save sex for marriage because He knows how powerful it is in the proper context. Sex works to cement the covenant relationship of marriage, but *outside of marriage it will cement a relationship that is not healthy*.

When a woman admits to me that she stayed with a Bozo for too long, I always ask, "Were you guys involved sexually?" The answer is always yes!

At a church event, one couple put on quite a tennis demonstration. This couple, who had been dating for a while, were playing a game of doubles. When the girl missed a few easy shots, the guy got so mad that he threw his tennis racket at his "girlfriend."

Those who saw this incident assumed that the girl would not be dating this guy anymore. Weeks later, two of the girls who had seen the angry outburst were stunned when they realized that this young man and woman were still together. I told them that only sex is powerful enough to blind a woman to the Bozo guy she is dating. Later we found out I was right.

From years of experience counseling thousands of broken-hearted women (young and old), I can assure you: sexual involvement puts leg irons on a woman and shackles her to a Bozo until he is finished using her. When the Bozo walks away, the leg irons are a bitter reminder of what she was willing to give sexually for love; but love was not what she got in return.

Sexual sin blurs your vision and leads you to mistake a Bozo for a Boaz—a mistake you may experience for a lifetime.

Beware of Cheering On the Bozo Tribe

Watch What You Wear

Sitting in the back of an auditorium in Buffalo, New York, I heard a young woman teaching about what I would call the cheerleading uniforms for Bozos. She explained that the way a girl dresses ultimately either encourages a male's purity or encourages his lust. She was challenging the teens to refuse to wear the typical Bozo cheerleading uniform of immodesty.

She shared an interesting statement that I think women need to consider whenever they either are getting dressed to go out or are shopping for a new outfit: people will treat you the way you are dressed. If you are dressed in a cheerleading uniform, you will be treated like and thought of as a cheerleader. If you are dressed in a police officer's uniform, you will be treated like and thought of as a police officer. So dress yourself the way you want to be treated! Matthew 12:34 says, "For out of the abundance of the heart the mouth speaks" (ESV). In the same way, your clothing speaks about what is in your heart.

The second point she made was taken from a great quote

from Justin Lookado, one of the authors of *Are You Dateable?* "If what you are showing ain't on the menu, keep it covered up!" She shared candidly about the reality of women, young and old, walking about displaying their private body parts as though they were the specials for the lunch menu that day!

I find it ironic that a woman will dress provocatively for a date but be insulted if the man wants to fondle what she has boldly displayed. A dear friend teaches on abstinence. She likens this behavior to placing a box of Krispy Kreme donuts on her chest. Then she talks about trying to hold a conversation with a starving man—without his wanting to paw the donut box. For a woman to display herself and expect a healthy man to not want to touch what is on display is so foolish.

My son, Ben, agrees: "Since I am a guy, I am really visual, so when a girl dresses like a hooker, it does not matter what comes out of her mouth . . . she has already told me all I want to know about her. The way girls dress—the more skin the guy sees—the less he is thinking about her as a person and the more she becomes an object. Guys have one-track minds. How [women] dress determines what track we get on. We're either on the get-to-know-you-as-a-person track or on the get-to-know-your-body track."

I read an article recently called "French Women Don't Get Painted Up." The writer referred to the present American look as "vulgar—a bit 'Desperate Housewife'-looking." To the French, American chic seems more suited for women in the famous Moulin Rouge.

Laura Mercier, French creator of a line of cosmetics, made a very sobering remark: "In America, even teenage girls are overly made-up. And when you are overly made-up, you send out the message that you are overly sexual, that you want to be visible to attract men."[1]

Mercier's comment just added to my concern about the message that teens and women in general are sending to the men around them. Whether it is their immodest clothing or their *"vulgaire"* makeup, both are communicating an "overly sexual" condition. Of course there is nothing wrong with wearing trendy clothes and good makeup to enhance the beauty within you. But you need to consider whether your clothes and cosmetics accentuate your true beauty or distract from the glow from within.

Immodest, distracting clothing is a Bozo cheerleading uniform.

Honor Your Body as a Temple

Look at what Paul wrote about sexual sin: "Flee from sexual immorality. All other sins a man commits are outside his body, but he who sins sexually sins against his own body. Do you not know that your body is a temple of the Holy Spirit, who is in you, whom you have received from God? You are not your own; you were bought at a price. Therefore honor God with your body" (1 Cor. 6:18–21).

One aspect of Paul's warning about sexual sin is the reality that our bodies were purchased by Jesus for God and they are now the very temples, dwelling places, of God's Holy Spirit. When Corinthian citizens visited the temples of their gods, they not only sacrificed to idols but also had encounters with temple prostitutes. Talk about perversion: religion and prostitution were a combo!

Paul's warning was powerful because the idea uniting the

very temple of God with a prostitute was horrifying. Although religion and prostitutes were, at the time, "politically correct," for the Christian it was an offensive sin against the very temple where God's Spirit was willing to dwell within us.

A single girl named Sylvia studied this passage to the Corinthians and was so captivated by the message that it profoundly impacted the way she dated from then on. When the next guy she dated rang the doorbell of her apartment, she answered and said, "I need to say something to you before we leave for our date." He replied, "Sure." She pointed at herself and said, "See this body? It is the temple of the Holy Spirit, and I need you to treat it accordingly."

Now, what was so ironic was that everyone in our singles' department at church knew about her great body. So for her to say, "See this body?" well, it was not hard to miss, but to add the instruction from the book written to the Cosmo Corinthians was absolutely the bomb!

On the late-night news I saw a clip from a local street in our town where hundreds of spring break college students had gathered. The clips showed girls who were being cheered on by the guys to pull up their shirts and expose their breasts. I wasn't totally surprised by the drunken cheers from the Bozo guys, but I was disappointed to see so many girls giving in to the suggestion to flaunt their "headlights."

Now, most Christian girls don't take off their shirts to expose their breasts on the news, but lately more and more Christian girls are taking the liberty to expose more and more of their bodies—imitating the world. This modern display of one's private parts not only is a lowering of a female's standards and manners, but also fuels the raging bonfire of lust that godly men are trying to battle. With the external overdose of cleavage window dressing, many men are considering it an unwinnable war.

Girls, listen to me. We want the men we care about to win this war against lust, but we need to be part of the solution and not part of the problem. Whenever another married woman is confiding in me about her husband's battle with pornography on the Internet, weeping about the shame she feels, I think of all the women who are utterly casual about displaying their body parts as single girls. However, once they are married, they want their husbands never to lust after another woman. Well, that training begins before marriage—through a few good women with the courage not to show their "headlights" and "taillights."

Be considerate of the man who is honestly trying to develop self-control, and understand that it begins with his eyes. You can help him become a Boaz—or not.

Avoid Verbal Foreplay

A way in which a woman can encourage a man in his battle to be self-controlled is to avoid "verbal foreplay." Author and speaker Josh McDowell was the first I heard use this term to describe intimate, emotional sharing. He warned that a couple's even praying together can lead to behavior that one would not expect in such a context. After all, praying is intimacy personified.

I know a couple who had gone to the best singles' Bible study in our town, then went back to the girl's apartment and, over coffee, began sharing. All that coffee helped prolong the chatting, and their verbal intimacy moved into sexual intimacy, and a baby girl was conceived that night.

Let me explain the idea a little more fully. A young woman is often used to sharing intimately with a girlfriend, and she assumes she can do the same with the guy she is dating. Well, she can share with a girlfriend for hours without her girlfriend wanting to make out with her. But when a girl shares deeply with a guy she is dating, too much intimate sharing can be like verbal foreplay. A handsome young man told me that when a girl shares very intimately with him, it is as though she is taking her blouse off in front of him.

I remember when my first Christian boyfriend was trying to explain to me why he was—get this!—still making out with his old girlfriend! He said, "She was devastated by a death in the family, and she was pouring her heart out to me, and after hours of listening . . . we were suddenly making out." My boyfriend was comforting his ex-girlfriend.

But, in fact, *I* was in need of comfort, because this betrayal, though it seemed minor to him, was devastating to me. I was a new Christian and had assumed that dating a Christian would be different. When I wasn't a follower of Jesus, I had dated several Bozo guys who fooled around with other girls while dating me. I had so much to learn about the character of a Boaz and the lack of character in a Bozo guy.

Don't be Bozo Bait by sharing too intimately with a guy. A Bozo will take advantage of this, and you'll face potentially devastating consequences.

Maintain Your Manners

While teaching at a college conference in Atlanta, I was getting ready to approach the podium to speak when the most beautiful girl walked in. I heard the oxygen being sucked out of the room when some of the guys gasped. The girl walked up to me and gave me a big hug and told me how excited she was to hear me teach girls how not to date a Bozo and teach guys how not to be one. I noticed the guys watching her as she walked away from me and took her seat in the audience.

As I shared the qualities of a Bozo, a guy to avoid, I also challenged the girls in the audience to not lower their standards of purity in order to get a guy—that is a sure way to become Bozo Bait. I told the girls that their standards inspire one of two things in the guys they know: lust or love for God. At the end of the conference I mentioned to my son the beautiful girl. My son remarked, "I know her. She is not just beautiful outside, she is even more beautiful inside. She is the kind of girl who makes a guy want to be God's best—a Boaz rather than a Bozo!" I thought, *May the tribe of God-inspiring girls increase!* Ben said later, "I have learned very quickly how fast a girl's beauty fades when she does not have a beautiful heart. A girl's heart gives her a beauty that will last her forever, long after the physical beauty has faded."

Internally beautiful girls hold powerful influence in the United States. This is a fact of culture that was observed as long ago as when the second president of the U.S., John Adams, made this empowering statement: "From all that I have read of history and government, of human life and manners, I have drawn this conclusion—the manners of women were the most infallible barometer to ascertain the degree of morality and virtue of a nation."

Now, consider the moral decay of our nation and consider the manners of leading female icons of our day—those who grace the covers of magazines, movie posters, and CD covers.

Do these females inspire lust or love for God? Then reflect for a moment the manners of the characters on nighttime soap operas such as *Sex and the City* and *Desperate Housewives*.

Let's not kid ourselves: isn't bold sexual activity what has given *Sex and the City* and *Desperate Housewives* such high Nielsen ratings? Aren't these shows popular because of the sexually stimulating conversations and explicit sexual activity? What exactly do such shows promote: holding out for a Boaz or becoming Bozo Bait and taking whatever comes our way?

Because the manners of women *are* such an infallible barometer, there is a direct correlation between the growth in the number of Bozos living among us and the number of desperate sex goddesses strewn throughout nighttime TV. Furthermore, this is the case not only in the story lines of shows, but also throughout the commercials. With so many girls lowering their standards to get a man, they have been instrumental in inducting thousands of women into becoming Bozo Bait and men into joining the Bozo Tribe.

To show this phenomenon in another, equally disturbing manifestation, I learned recently that junior high girls are now making out with other girls at parties in order to send a signal to the guys that they are easy. Question: where on earth would a junior high girl see women making out with women just to sensationalize their sexually free spirits? Well, we have the infamous example of Madonna, Christina, and Britney on the MTV Awards, but you can add to that any number of images currently in the movies, which have served to normalize this trend in sexual behavior.

When women lower their standards, men assume that being a Bozo is not so bad after all because, frankly, there are no negative consequences for their behavior. In fact, they feel egged on! That is why the Bozo tribe has grown during the last four decades; women keep abandoning their ideals and becoming bait for the very guys they ought to avoid like the plague.

> Who has influenced my ideals the most as a man? My wife, Sandy.
> —Gary Carter, Baseball Hall of Famer

My brother-in-law heard on the radio an expert saying that in different cultures, it has been noted that men were not civilized until they got married. Men need women in more ways than one . . . women need not lower their standards and abort a man's chance to grow up. Just last week I was reading an article in *People* magazine that was titled: "They Really, Really, Need a Woman." I just smiled when I read the title, because I know that God made women to bless men and complement them. Just remember that Adam and God had a perfect relationship before Eve was created. But in that perfection, it was not good for Adam to be alone—God knew he needed a suitable journey partner. So He created women—and one of our roles is to uphold our standards.

Just Say No

When a woman uses the word *no*, she requires a man to exercise the self-control that God wants him to develop. Her *no* builds the character of this Man Worth Waiting For—a man of strength—a modern Boaz.

A single guy controlling himself sexually is a greater accomplishment than a steroid-filled, pumped-up professional athlete who hits a grand slam. Single men do not die if they don't have sex regularly. There is a lie that has circulated among most men since their teens that they must have a certain amount of sex or they will face the DSBs (deadly sperm buildup). The DSBs actually are controlled through abstinence. Abstinence is not agonizing deprivation but a challenge on Olympic competition level.

The development of self-control impacts not only sex but also every other pleasurable interest in life. A rite of passage often neglected in America is the capacity to postpone what you want for a greater good. Newborn babies only know what they need *now*, and they scream to get what they want. We anticipate that, as the child grows, the screaming will subside and patience will develop. When an adult is demanding his desires be satisfied *now*, he has continued in a prolonged infancy and thinks that postponing the fulfillment of desires is not possible.

No is a gift you give to a man that you care about, just as his respect for your response is a gift to you. In his book *To Own a Dragon*, Don Miller validates my remarks: "Women saying no to men, not letting men have sex with them, causes men to step up. . . . I think men need women to be women, and we need to be made to jump through some hoops. If a woman withholds sex until she gets what she wants, we are all better for it."[2] A girl is actually blessing her guy when she says no. She is enhancing his inner world and strengthening his potential to leave his adolescence.

So, to help with the civilizing of men, stop cheering for the Bozo tribe. Stop validating their distorted view of sex by compromising your moral ideals. I have a friend that didn't want to wear the typical purity ring. She wanted something trendier than a ring symbolic of her keeping her virginity until she got married. What did she do? She had her belly button pierced with a blue gemstone. The blue stone was because of the "blue cord" that was to be a reminder to obey.

> Throughout the generations to come you are to make tassels on the corners of your garments with a *blue cord* on each tassel. You will have these tassels to look at and so you will remember all the commands of the LORD, that you may obey them and not prostitute yourselves by going after the lusts of your own hearts and eyes. (Numbers 15:37–39, italics mine)

Even before a couple starts to date seriously, the guy needs to practice saying no to Miss Lust so that he can resist her tempting voice after the wedding day.

Again, for a woman, young or old, the sobering power of "no" is the greatest gift she can give to her man. Every time she says no, she is cheering on his capacity to control his own body in honor of God's glory. Every time she says no, she is helping a Boaz stay strong, or she is refusing to be Bozo Bait for someone who will use her, then move on.

Beware of Our Culture's Bozo Dating Standards

Too many Christian girls have at the core of their hearts Hollywood's dating standards rather than biblical truths for discerning good dating partners. Christians think that if they take the romantic standards they have gleaned from a hundred chick flicks and blend them with a couple of Bible verses, they will avoid Bozo guys and find God's best.

An especially important and basic guideline has to do with dating nonbelievers. I am absolutely stunned that so many Christian girls totally disregard the warning in God's Word about dating Bozos: "Do not be yoked together with unbelievers. For what do righteousness and wickedness have in common? Or what fellowship can light have with darkness?" (2 Cor. 6:14). I was shocked the first time I found out that a wonderful Christian girl who led my Bible study each week was dating a non-Christian. What was she thinking? How could she ignore the advice of the ultimate Lover of her soul and give up her ideals of God's best in a guy? Ultimately this young woman was using worldly dating standards—date the best guy you can find, regardless of his spiritual condition—rather than God's.

Some may ask, is it okay to date a moral guy who is not a Christian? My answer: why would you want to date someone who doesn't love Jesus the way you do? Such a spiritual mismatch will lead only to heartache (Amos 3:3; Mal. 2:15; Josh. 23:12–14). You want to date a guy whose heart Jesus has freedom to influence.

Considering that Americans' dating standards are more culturally than biblically driven, the divorce rate among Christians isn't surprising. The morbid statistics concerning divorce—about half of all marriages fail—no longer exclude believers. Christian girls choose Bozo guys because they are driven more by the mental pictures of the last ten romantic comedies they have seen rather than guided by the God of the universe, who alone knows the men for whom they are suitable journey partners. *A Man Worth Waiting For will be found only by a woman who waits!*

I know single girls who have no problem watching soap operas, whether during the day or at night, but they don't have even fifteen minutes to spend in God's Love Manual, His Word. Throughout the Bible we are encouraged to not let the Word slip away from us (Deut. 4:9; Jer. 15:16; Job 23:12; Heb. 4:12). We have exchanged the Word of God for the remote control for our TV or even our DVD player, where we are playing our favorite chick flick for the twenty-fifth time.

To enhance your mastery of God's Word, you need not only a daily time reading the Love Manual, but also a Bible study, small group, or Sunday school class where you can deepen your grasp of the truths in God's Word. There are so many golden nuggets of truth to be mined.

Being driven more by culture than by the ultimate Love Manual makes you easy Bozo Bait, which makes you terribly vulnerable to bad relationships. To find God's best and resist the Bozo, you need to be grounded in biblical truths, not Hollywood fantasies. This biblical core will form an internal radar system that alerts you quickly to Bozos and will sustain you as you hold out for a Boaz—the Man Worth Waiting For. The Bible's "instructions are not mere words—they are your life!" (Deut. 32:47 NLT).

DISCUSSION QUESTIONS

- ✿ When have you been most tempted to give up your ideals? *Psalm 84:11–12*
- ✿ Have you been a willing cheerleader for the Bozos in your life?
- ✿ Has this cheering been a recent event or was it part of your

past? If you have stopped cheering for the Bozo tribe, what made you stop?

♧ Have you ever been a Bozo Magnet? *Amos 3:3* Why?

♧ Discuss the premise that sexual involvement blurs your heart's vision. Have you seen this in the life of a friend—or in yourself?

♧ What did you think about the French woman's opinion that American women often dress in an overtly sexual way? Does it inspire you or offend you?

♧ Before you are tempted to consider dating a non-Christian guy, read these verses: *Joshua 23:12–14; 2 Corinthians 6:14.* Why is a good, moral guy—but a non-Christian—not a good choice?

☙ 12

be kind to your heart

Where is your heart right this moment? Are you content, or are you tapping your foot and looking at your watch that says "a quarter past thirty"? Are you worried about your biological clock ticking too loud? Are you checking out "meet markets," scanning every guy you see for Boaz material, dreaming over wedding rings in jewelry ads?

Such anxious thoughts will drive you to be reckless with your own heart. The Bible warns against this: "Above all else, guard your heart, for it is the wellspring of life" (Prov. 4:23). This verse states that a person's *number-one priority* should be protecting her heart. This applies not only to single women who are living in prolonged singleness but to every person living. To "guard your heart" is to inspect it as you would inspect a garden for weeds. How quickly weeds spring up and destroy the beauty in a garden. Trust me, weeds of discontentment can strangle a woman's heart as quickly as weeds strangle beautiful plants.

When a woman doesn't inspect her heart and guard it like a precious, secret garden, she is more prone to break what I called in *Lady in Waiting* "the eleventh commandment."

Guard Your Heart from Fantasies

The "eleventh commandment" is this: *Defraud not thyself, harming oneself through one's fantasy life.* When I talk with single girls across the U.S., they all admit they have a tendency to defraud themselves—lead themselves on through fantasies about the most eligible bachelors in their lives.

Consider how often women are angry about a particular guy's leading his girlfriend on in a dating relationship—often the result of a guy's agenda to play at love to get sex. I wonder how often a single woman (young or old) gets angry with herself for letting her mind and heart wander beyond the real level of commitment between her and the guy she's interested in. How often do single women get angry with their girlfriends who helped feed the fantasy about "Mr. Right"?

> Friends too often participate in the development of one's prenuptial fantasies. After only one date with a wonderful man, a girl will share the details of the evening and her friends will not only share her joy, but also foster excessive imaginings by asking questions like, "Do you think this is the one?" We not only need the discipline of monitoring our own fantasies, but we also need friends who will remind us not to run ahead of God's timing. Such monitoring of our emotions and accountability

between friends is so helpful for the Christian single woman.

Ironically, the same close friends who help to accelerate the prenuptial fantasy may be the ones who must comfort the lone lovebird when Mr. Right asks another girl out and no more history is to be made with him. Her disappointment will be in direct proportion to the degree that she and her friends responded prematurely to a relationship that will last only in her memory. The next time a friend shares the details of an exciting evening with such a hunk of a guy, don't overreact. Instead, say to her, "I am thrilled that you had a great time. I am so glad you shared your excitement with me. Now do yourself a favor and before you close your eyes to dream tonight, prayerfully commit Mr. Wonderful to Jesus." You will be a true friend and a spiritual monitor for her.[1]

Greg Behrendt and Liz Tuccillo wrote a popular book titled *He's Just Not That into You*. This is what I have been telling hundreds of singles during the last three decades: *stop leading yourself into prenuptial fantasies.* Guard your heart! If he truly "is not that into you," the passion you feel and the relentless pursuit you want to act out are more in your heart than his. That is a warning sign! A Man Worth Waiting For will match your passion. A Bozo will let you love him as much as you want—without ever returning the affection.

Guard Your Heart from a Lack of *Boule*

In the book of Deuteronomy, several passages refer to the failure to act wisely. For example, "Israel is a nation that lacks sense" (Deut. 32:28).[2] When I looked closely at the word trans-lated "sense," I discovered the Greek word *boule,* which refers to the counsel that precedes good decision making. I immedi-ately thought of "Bozo and No *Boule*"—B&B. The words are a perfect combo, like salt and pepper! Then I began to think of all the wonderful girls who have stayed too long at this "B&B" where their hearts have been broken and they live in a con-tinual nightmare on Bozo Street. A good friend will help you guard your heart against Bozos and all their lack of *boule*.

Recently I asked a friend about her beloved daughter's boy-friend and she said, "I don't think he is a good fit. He is so self-ish and so demanding—but she can't see it." Here is another precious girl who is staying at the "B&B" with her heart already scheduled for pain. "Bozo and No *Boule*" guarantees heart-break. Here a girl had a wise friend—her mother—but failed to heed her counsel.

In every heartbreaking story I hear, a girl ignored the cau-tions of a parent or a friend. To date a Bozo, a girl must ig-nore *boule*—good advice. Consider the first woman who ever lived, the *boule* she ignored, and the price she paid. So has every Evette ever since!

If you have a good friendship with a wonderful single guy, you need a friend to whom you are accountable about guard-ing your heart against premature dreams of a future with this guy. This will help you develop the habit of thinking and acting wisely in regard to the men in your life. Proverbs says, "If you reprove the wise, they will be all the wiser" (Prov. 19:25 NLT). I hope you have a friend who knows how to shoot "*boule* arrows" into your heart should you be tempted to succumb to a Bozo's influence. "Wounds from a friend can be trusted" (Prov. 27:6).

If you don't have a friend with the courage to shoot *boule* arrows into your distracted heart, then start praying for one. All women need to "deputize a Nathan" to speak the truth to them when their hearts are deceived. (Remember, Nathan was the prophet God sent to speak strong truth to deceived King David after David committed adultery and murder.)

I have been blessed with several "Nathans" during the last four decades of my walk with Jesus. These friends have kept me from disastrous decisions that would have altered the whole direction of my life. Guard your heart from bad decisions. Find yourself a reliable friend, and let her help you keep your thoughts and fantasies on track.

Guard Your Heart: Put Your Passion into Prayer

Too many single women's tears are the result of their not guarding their hearts in relation to the men they admire.

If you admire a certain guy, guard your heart by taking *every* thought about him to Jesus in prayer. It is a win-win situation when you pray for those you admire. Pray for God's best for him, and don't add your name to the "best" column. The unselfish act of prayer on his behalf will help to purify your heart in relation to God's script for the situation. "The LORD's searchlight penetrates the human spirit, exposing every hidden motive" (Prov. 20:27 NLT).

It is time to say the Single Woman's Pledge of Allegiance. Place your hand over your heart and repeat after me:

By God's grace I will guard my heart daily.
I will endeavor to faithfully keep the Eleventh Commandment—

I will not allow my mind to harm me through Knight in Shining Armor fantasies.

I will find someone to hold me accountable to this pledge and to God's plan for my life.

I will wait for God's Boaz, and I will be honest with myself about the Bozos I meet along the way.

I will become a Woman Worth Waiting For as I await God's best for me.

Guard Your Heart Against the Commitment-Phobic

Once I asked an eligible bachelor why he was still single. He said, "Do you want a spiritual answer or an honest answer?" I said, "Honest, please." His reply has been etched on my heart for two decades: "I could have told you that I have been single because of a noble purpose for God, but I think my singleness has been prolonged because I am not ready to give up life on *my terms.*"

This is true of all of us at one time or another. But Bozos are bent on their wants and ways—they will ultimately reject anything that threatens their selfish lifestyles. If you find yourself in a relationship where you're doing all the giving, compromising, and sacrificing, you've found yourself a Bozo. Make no mistake: commitment-phobic guys will end up hurting you if you invest your heart in any of them.

Guard Your Heart Against the "Cult of Quick"

Sometimes when a woman thinks her singleness has dragged on for too long, her impatience and the corresponding defrauding can wear down the battery on her Bozo Alert. Her alarm doesn't sound when she begins dating a Bozo even though her friends can clearly see the Bozo characteristics.

The fact is, though, Christian singles are influenced more by our culture than they are by the Bible. Our culture wants everything instant and express. Such an attitude results in a compromise of character, and a Man Worth Waiting For has character that is developed only over time. Countless women settle for half-baked character in the guys they date.

I had a very precious friend who, after a long season of date-lessness, began to date a guy whom all her friends, except me, considered a catch. I knew that no one agreed with my opinion, so I began to pray for my friend. I could tell her Bozo Alert system was not functioning and that she was in danger of committing a lifelong error. I was so disappointed that all her friends were cheering on her relationship with a Bozo, whose main attraction was his good looks.

When word came that she was engaged, I prayed even more fervently. I asked that something would happen that would shock her to the core, and that even though her Bozo Alert had malfunctioned, somehow she would see the guy for the Bozo he was. After months of praying and many tears shed for my friend, I heard one Valentine's Day that she had broken the engagement. None of her friends, except me, understood the good news this was.

Years later, when I was the matron of honor in her wedding, I wept throughout the ceremony as I witnessed her marrying the Boaz that God had for her—my brother-in-law Gary. My best friend of thirty-two years was now my sister-in-law.

Don't let a broken Bozo Alert usher you into joining the Cult of Quick. This ever-present attitude in the U.S. encourages too many women to rush into relationships. The Cult of Quick does not give a woman enough time to find her heart's complement in a man. Whenever I hear about a couple meeting, quickly getting engaged, and then quickly marrying, I cringe. I know there are some wonderful exceptions to the old saying "Quick to the altar, quick to divorce"—but as a rule, the Cult of Quick escorts more women into disaster than it does into "happily ever after."

We are all acquainted with the expression "Speed kills." Although this expression was a warning for driving too fast in one's car, the principle is true in the matters of the heart, because speed kills on the relational highway. In the area of lust, there is only one speed limit—fast. There is no constraining governor on the gas pedal! Guard your heart from the Cult of Quick—and the miserable destination it will lead to.

Let's look at a biblical illustration of this. The story of foot-tapping impatience centers on a man named Achan (are you impatiently "achin'" for a man?) in the book of Joshua. Upon first reading this story, you may think it is a simple story of a man's lusting after the spoils of a conquered city (Jericho). But there's a deeper issue at work.

We read that God gave explicit instructions before the battle about the city's wealth: "All the silver and gold and the articles of bronze and iron are sacred to the LORD and must go into his treasury." God even outlined the consequences of ignoring this command: "Keep away from the devoted things, so that you will not bring about your own destruction by taking any of them. Otherwise you will make the camp of Israel liable to destruction and bring trouble on it" (Josh. 6:19, 18).

Yet we read, "The Israelites acted unfaithfully in regard to the devoted things; Achan son of Carmi, . . . of the tribe of Judah, took some of them. So the LORD's anger burned against Israel" (Josh. 7:1). Achan's sneaky behavior was a direct violation of God's instruction, but there is another aspect of the tragedy. Achan's sin was not only greed but the deeper sin of presumption. Achan assumed that he wouldn't have what he needed in the Promised Land—so he stole.

When God gave the marching orders for Jericho, He said, "No plunder for the warriors." Being a warrior, Achan presumed that "no plunder for the warriors" would be the marching orders for all the cities the Israelites would conquer. So Achan gave in to his cravings, assuming God would not provide for him as a warrior. Sadly, Achan stole in Jericho what God was going to freely give him in the next city of Ai. *Achan took what God would have given him if Achan had only trusted God's timing and specific marching orders.*

The result? The next time Israel went to conquer a city, the army failed miserably: "They were routed by the men of Ai, who . . . chased the Israelites from the city gate as far as the stone quarries and struck them down on the slopes. At this the hearts of the people melted and became like water" (Josh. 7:4–5). When Joshua protested to the Lord, God explained why He didn't support His people in battle: "They have taken some of the devoted things; they have stolen, they have lied, they have put them with their own possessions. That is why the Israelites cannot stand against their enemies; they turn their backs and run because they have been made liable to destruction" (Josh. 7:11–12). Ultimately Achan's sin cost his life, his family's lives, and the lives of the warriors who failed in the battle with Ai.

Impatience can generate far-reaching disaster.

So many single girls "steal" any man they can find—typically a Bozo—because they assume that God will not bring Mr. Right into their lives. What about you? Are you presently living with anxiety about your prolonged singleness? Are you discouraged by a drought of datelessness? Put your hope in God, and wait patiently for what He will freely provide. Ask God to forgive you for living even a moment of life drenched in fear rather than drenched in faith. And focus on becoming a Woman Worth Waiting For.

Guard Your Heart Against Taking Someone Else's Boaz

Too often when a single girl has been very patient for an extended period of time, she is more vulnerable than ever when she *finally meets a Boaz*. He may have just moved into the circle of friends that she associates with daily. He may have just been transferred into the office where she works. He may have been invited as a guest to a singles' Bible study she is attending. No matter how he arrives—even if it is on a white horse and he is wearing Knight's Armor Cologne—a woman still must guard her heart against the ever-prevalent assumption that he is "the" Boaz she has been waiting for.

After her first conversation with this modern Boaz, the moment she is alone, she needs to put her hand over her heart and say the Single Woman's Pledge of Allegiance. She needs to make herself accountable to a friend. She needs to devote herself to prayer about the great man she has just met.

You may think I'm recommending extreme reactions. "If

he's a Boaz," you reason, "why not just grab him?" To guard your heart when "Mr. Right" arrives within ten feet of you may seem unnecessary, but countless women have lived with the deepest of heart wounds because they assumed that a great guy was *the* MWWF. *But just because he is a Boaz doesn't mean he is your Boaz.*

Just before I left for college, a young man spoke at our home Bible study. We were all so impressed with this good-looking guy who was not ashamed of his passion for God. That night several of us left the study with a bit of a crush on this godly young man. He was an obvious Boaz.

When I returned to college, I was stunned to find a letter from him. He began to write to me regularly. His deep love for God permeated his letters. After writing me for several months, he came to visit me at college in Chattanooga. I was so nervous, because I knew what an incredible guy he was and I honestly was shocked by his interest in me.

He stayed with a guy friend of mine in the men's dorm, and we spent every free moment throughout the weekend together. Just before he was ready to return to his job in Atlanta, we took a walk and he said, "Jackie, I have been praying for months and I have spoken with my parents about this—I believe that you are the woman I have been waiting for all these years." He said he would drive back to see me in three weeks and I could tell him how I felt about him at that time.

Less than twenty-four hours later, I was thinking about our time together and what an incredible guy he was. While I was praying, I heard, "Yes, he is incredible, but he is not your Boaz." I recommitted myself to God's plan, and I immediately wrote and told the young man he didn't need to return in three weeks.

I told him that God showed me clearly that he was not my Boaz. In fact, I closed my letter with this comment: "Adam, go back to sleep, your Eve is not ready yet."

That may seem harsh, but wait 'til you hear the rest of the story.

With my rejection of this Boaz's proposal, he agreed to join the God's Smuggler team with its leader, Brother Andrew, in Europe. This group smuggled Bibles into Communist countries when it was illegal—and very dangerous—to do so. For ten years, this Boaz served with that team. His singleness was a great advantage. He could serve with Brother Andrew in hazardous situations without worries for a wife and children. The inherent risks that came daily with this particular work would have put enormous pressure on any team member who was married.

I said no to Boaz, and he was free to take risks serving the Lord he loved so desperately. Yes, he was a Boaz, but he was not mine, and I was not his Ruth.

After serving for ten years, he returned to Atlanta where he finally married his Ruth. I eventually met my Boaz, Ken, and married him. The next time you meet an obvious Boaz, pray that he finds his Ruth—even if it is not you.

Guard Your Heart Against the Technological "Meet Market"

Many singles complain about the typical "meet markets" at their church and opt for something available only in the last couple of decades: Internet dating. I call this a "technological meet market." Some have found meeting men that way useful; others have experienced only more disappointment. Here's what my friend Jennie said:

> Internet dating was a good learning experience. I had a friend who works in our corporate office meet her husband via an online dating service. She's a huge proponent of Internet dating and after hearing her encouragement, I couldn't help but consider it.
>
> I didn't enter the Internet dating scene expecting the love of my life to pop up on e-mail (although I wanted to be open to it), but I did think that it would be a good opportunity to meet men that I wouldn't normally cross paths with or consider.
>
> But when I did date some guys from the online matchmaking service, I met a few guys who were socially awkward, a very wealthy guy who didn't have a strong relationship with the Lord, one that I wasn't at all attracted to physically, and only one that I thought had potential—in the end, it didn't work out.

As you can see, online dating has different results for everyone. I have just two cautionary thoughts about this technological meet market. First, Internet meeting is a very seductive place for fantasy-forming precisely because you have built-in distance and can mentally make a man into something he may not be at all! Second, if a woman's Bozo Alert isn't functioning and she doesn't know it, or if she has no *boule* friends who can help steer her actions, she can get connected to someone without anyone around her knowing about it. Then she's free to justify a lot of things that seem innocent because the whole relationship is virtual. Yet none of her emotions are virtual!

Jennie made the interesting point that online dating gave her opportunities to meet men that she might not usually encounter. But she approached the experience with the right attitude: she was open but not expectant. If you are guarding your heart, you will approach the technological meet market the same way.

Guard Your Heart Against the Lie That Only Singles Are Lonely

In the mid-1800s, a lovely single woman wrote to author Hannah Whitall Smith about her struggle with loneliness and depression. You may have heard Hannah's name before—she wrote the classic *The Christian's Secret of a Happy Life*. The answer she gave her lonely friend is just as relevant now as it was in the nineteenth century.

> The loneliness thou speaks of I know all about. For do not think, darling, that it is confined to unmarried people. It is just as real in lives that have plenty of human ties: husbands and children and friends. . . . And I believe God very rarely allows any human love to be satisfying, just that this loneliness may drive us to Himself. I have noticed that where a human love is satisfying, something always comes in to spoil it. Either there is a death, or there are separations, or there is change of feeling on one side or the other, or something, and the heart is driven out of its human resting place.[3]

An e-mail I received from a precious single girl living in the Middle East named Keren reminded me of what Hannah wrote. She clearly understands the commitment required from a single woman who wants to guard her heart and follow her God. Keren wrote:

> I can read the Bible a hundred times, read *Lady in Waiting* fifty times, but if my heart is not ready to give away to Him my desires, nothing in the world will help. Therefore it is for those who are ready to give the King all their dreams, desires, and wishes and go with their "Naomis" to the unknown [that they will find] in the end God's promised land. [Such following may] look good to us or not—but God, His ways are perfect, and He protects those who hide under the shadow of His wings. We must trust God during our time of waiting, during moments of loneliness, and must fight the best we can (with God's help) to guard our hearts, for from our hearts come the issues of life.

In her letter to the single woman, Hannah Whitall Smith went one step further to remind her—and all of us, single, married, widowed, divorced—that the ultimate answer is not in Mr. Right but in a right relationship with God. In this excerpt, Hannah addressed the timeless reality that *God is enough*.

> No soul can be really at rest until it has given up all dependence on everything else and has been forced to depend on the Lord alone. As long as our expectation is from other things, nothing but disappointment awaits us. Feelings may change, and will change, with our changing circumstances: doctrines and dogmas may be upset; Christian work may come to naught; prayers may

seem to lose their fervency; promises may seem to fail; everything that we have believed in or depended upon may seem to be swept away, and only God is left, just God, the bare God, if I may be allowed the expression; simply and only God. . . .

This, then, is what I mean by God being enough. It is that we find in Him, the fact of His existence and of His character, all that we can possibly want for everything. God is, must be, our answer to every question and every cry of need. If there is any lack in the One who has undertaken to save us, nothing supplementary we can do will avail to make it up; and if there is no lack in Him, then He of Himself and in Himself is enough.[4]

Guard Your Heart Against Demanding Your Way

Contentment is always a miracle for a woman, no matter what her marital status. Being satisfied and at peace comes only when a woman has learned the secret to all miracles, which is saying a holy "Whatever, Lord." Let me explain.

In the familiar Christmas story passage in the Gospel of Luke, we read of a miracle that occurred before Jesus' actual birth: it was a young girl's response to this daunting heavenly assignment. When the angel told Mary what God wanted her to do—to carry the body of His only Son, no less—Mary said, "I am the Lord's servant, and I am willing to accept *whatever* He wants" (Luke 1:38 NLT, italics mine).

To a casual observer, Mary's "whatever" may not seem very impressive, but her response reflected the surrender necessary for the greatest miracle: a virgin would conceive Emmanuel. Mary's holy "Whatever, Lord" ushered in God's physical presence on earth and brought her such honor—mothering the blessed Lamb of God.

I believe that every miracle is preceded by a holy "Whatever" of surrender. I wonder how many miracles single women miss because they don't surrender to God's script—instead they demand their own way and plans.

As a teenager, Mary of Nazareth set a precedent for all women to follow. Pray for a heart attitude like Mary's and get ready for more miracles than ever as you humbly yield to God's best. In doing so, you protect your heart from hardening due to bitterness when life and love don't go as well as they could. You guard your heart from despair.

You can live content today without your Boaz as you practice the holy "Whatever You say, Lord."

So, as you wait for the man worth all your effort, be kind to your heart by protecting it as if it is precious—because it is.

DISCUSSION QUESTIONS

- ☘ Can you think of an example of a friend defrauding herself in relation to a single guy she is attracted to? What happened when she realized her fantasies were just that—fantasies?
- ☘ Discuss how easy it is to lead yourself on through prenuptial fantasies. Is this practice a snare for you? Why?
- ☘ Discuss the self-defrauding that the title of a popular book exposed: *He's Just Not That into You.*
- ☘ Since male-female communication is often a collision course, what limits can you set on sharing your feelings and thoughts with a man?

✿ Discuss this idea: Just because he is a Boaz doesn't mean he's your Boaz.

✿ Have you ever assumed a Boaz was yours? What happened when you realized you were wrong?

✿ Discuss the cautions you need to take when entering the Technological Meet Market.

✿ Is Hannah W. Smith's statement that "God is enough" too high an ideal even to comprehend? Are you learning and practicing this truth as a single girl?

✿ Do you think contentment requires a daily miracle? When you are restless, how do you calm down and regain your peace? *Luke 1:37–38; Philippians 4:11–12*

✿ Look at Joshua 7 and answer these questions in relation to Achan's impatience.

✓ How often do you steal too early what God later wants to give you freely? *Romans 8:32*

✓ How often do you impatiently pursue what your Father wants to give you as you are sitting still? *Isaiah 64:4*

✓ How often do you panic and conclude that God is not going to provide a Boaz for you? *Matthew 6:25–33*

✓ How often do we assume what God is going to do next and we rush ahead, fearful that it will not satisfy us? Are you trying to help God find your Mr. Right?

✓ How many times have you suffered because you assumed what God would do and then you were knocked down by the surprise turn of events? *Isaiah 55:8–9*

✓ What will you do to build up your patience?

✿ a final note

who is writing your love story?

We women sure love love. The current label for a twenty-first-century love story is a "chick flick" or "chick lit." Whatever these stories are called, why do women get excited about reading or seeing a new love story played out on pages or on the big screen—whereas a man groans at the prospect of having to sit through another one? Why is a woman willing to sit through a bloody battle between the Scots and the English (theme of the movie *Braveheart*) in order to see a few moments of a tender love story? The answers are simple: Love to a woman is her whole life. Love to a man is only part of his life.

When I was in college studying literature, again and again I read about love being the center of a woman's world. Even in Paul's famous passage about the roles of men and women in marriage (Eph. 5), he didn't command a woman to love her husband but he did command the husband to love his wife. Why? Love for a man is too often a vague reality, but for a woman, it is as bright as a sunrise over the ocean.

> *It ever has been since time began,*
> *And ever will be, till time lose breath,*
> *That love is a mood—no more—to a man,*
> *And love to a woman is life or death.*

Ella Wheeler Wilcox (1850–1919) captured in those four lines a woman's hunger to love and be loved. This love hunger is often the very thing that causes a woman to embrace the prospect of being loved—even if it is by a Bozo—rather than face a prolonged wait for a Boaz.

I know you have that love hunger, or you wouldn't have picked up this book. I ask you today: who is writing your love story: you or God? After reading all these pages, are you willing to wait for God's best, or would you rather settle for a guy you pick out just because you're tired of waiting? I hope you've been enveloped in the love of God as you've read and become convinced that only One person knows what—and who—is really right for you.

As a young woman, I was such a romantic, and God used the leading man in the book of Ruth to introduce me to a sacred romance that surpassed anything I ever read about in literature. For me, Ruth presented a love story that beats all the love stories written since! The good news is: God is still writing love stories.

The One who wrote the first love story will also be the Author of the last love story. God's love for mankind was the first love story in the book of Genesis, and the last love story is already recorded in the last book of the Bible. The story includes a big wedding, and those who love God and are loved by God will be His Bride at the elaborate Marriage Feast of the Lamb to be held in eternity future.

Dear reader, let God write your love story. Let Him surpass all your expectations with a Man truly Worth Waiting For. Let Him bring you your own Boaz, and your love story will be as powerful as his was!

notes

1. the original MWWF

1. Spiros Zodhiates, ed., *Key Word Study Bible* (Chattanooga, TN: AMG Publishers, 1996), 575.

2. is the MWWF an extinct ideal?

1. Haley and Michael DiMarco, *Marriable: Taking the Desperate Out of Dating* (Grand Rapids, MI: Fleming H. Revell, a division of Baker Publishing Group, 2005), 127. Used by permission of Baker Publishing Group.

3. the counterfeit of a MWWF

1. John R. Kohlenberger III and James A. Swanson, *A Concise Dictionary of the Greek* (Grand Rapids, MI: Zondervan, 1996), 2117, #5408.

2. Jackie Kendall and Debby Jones, *Lady in Waiting* (Shippensburg, PA: Destiny Image Publishers, 1995), 148, and Jackie Kendall, *Say Goodbye to Shame* (Shippensburg, PA: Destiny Image Publishers, 2005). Used by permission of Destiny Image Publishers.

3. *Merriam-Webster's Collegiate Dictionary*, 11th ed. (Springfield, MA: Merriam-Webster, Inc., 2003), 148.

4. *The Oxford American College Dictionary* (New York: G. P. Putnam's Sons, 2002), 163.

5. *Strong's Exhaustive Concordance* (McLean, VA: MacDonald Publishing Co., 1972), 31, #1937.

6. Ibid., 9, #137.

7. Dr. Gwin Turner, *The Heritage Bible*, http://www.cathedraluniversity.com/heritagebible/index.asp.

8. John R. Kohlenberger III and James A. Swanson, *A Concise Dictionary of the Hebrew* (Grand Rapids, MI: Zondervan, 1996), 645, #586.

9. Ibid., 1976, #5572.

4. farmers and princes

1. *Strong's*, 133, #1162.

2. Turner, *Heritage Bible*, http://www.cathedraluniversity.com/heritagebible/HeritageBibleAcrobat/08Ruth.pdf.

3. *Strong's*, 76, #5037.

4. Ibid., 20, #1108.

7. courage in suffering

1. *Heritage Bible*, http://www.cathedraluniversity.com/heritagebible/HeritageBibleAcrobat/10Samuel2.pdf.

2. Ann Kiemel Anderson, *This Is a Story about God* (Kansas City, MO: Beacon Hill Press of Kansas City, 1998), 68. Used by permission of Beacon Hill Press of Kansas City. All rights reserved.

8. reckless abandon

1. Oswald Chambers, *My Utmost for His Highest* (Uhrichsville, OH: Barbour Publishing, 1963).

2. Erwin R. McManus, *The Barbarian Way* (Nashville, TN: Thomas Nelson Publishing, 2005), 66.

3. John Piper, *The Legacy of Sovereign Joy: God's Triumphant Grace in the Lives of Augustine, Luther, and Calvin* (Wheaton, IL: Crossway Books, a di-

vision of Good News Publishers, 2000). Used by permission of Crossway Books, a publishing ministry of Good News Publishers. You can visit John Piper's Web site at www.desiringGod.org.

4. Quoted in Joshua Harris, *Stop Dating the Church* (Sisters, OR: Multnomah Press, 2004), 106.

9. faithful though flawed

1. Piper, *Legacy*.

2. *Strong's*, 10, #223.

3. Chuck and Barb Snyder, *Incompatibility: Still Grounds for a Great Marriage* (Sisters, OR: Multnomah Press, 1994).

4. "Martin Luther," http://www.greatsite.com/timeline-english-bible-history/martin-luther.html.

10. surrounded by good company

1. *Strong's*, 41, #2698; 87, #5838; 65, #4332.

11. don't be bozo bait

1. David Seitz, "French Women Don't Get Painted Up," *Palm Beach Post*, June 1, 2006, Accent section.

2. Donald Miller, *To Own a Dragon* (Colorado Springs, CO: NavPress, 2006), 139.

12. be kind to your heart

1. Kendall and Jones, *Lady in Waiting*, 126. Used by permission of Destiny Image Publishers.

2. Zodhiates, *Key Word Study Bible*.

3. Marie Henry, *Hannah Whitall Smith* (Grand Rapids, MI: Bethany House, a division of Baker Book House, 1993). Used by permission of Baker Publishing Group. Quotes originally from Hannah Whitall Smith, *The Unselfishness of God* (Uhrichsville, OH: Barbour Publishing, n.d.). Used by permission.

4. Ibid.

about the author

Jackie Kendall has been a sought-after conference speaker for thirty years. As president of Power to Grow Ministries, Jackie speaks to people of all ages and stages of life (including, since 1992, professional baseball and football players). Jackie is the coauthor of the bestselling *Lady in Waiting*.

To contact Jackie Kendall for speaking engagements or to get more information, see:

Power to Grow Ministries
www.jackiekendall.com